The Best
Men's Stage Monologues
of 1992

Smith and Kraus *Books For Actors*
THE MONOLOGUE SERIES
The Best Men's / Women's Stage Monologues of 1994
The Best Men's / Women's Stage Monologues of 1993
The Best Men's / Women's Stage Monologues of 1992
The Best Men's / Women's Stage Monologues of 1991
The Best Men's / Women's Stage Monologues of 1990
One Hundred Men's / Women's Stage Monologues from the 1980's
2 Minutes and Under: Character Monologues for Actors
Street Talk: Character Monologues for Actors
Uptown: Character Monologues for Actors
Monologues from Contemporary Literature: Volume I
Monologues from Classic Plays
100 Great Monologues from the Renaissance Theatre
100 Great Monologues from the Neo-Classical Theatre
100 Great Monologues from the 19th C. Romantic and Realistic Theatres

FESTIVAL MONOLOGUE SERIES
The Great Monologues from the Humana Festival
The Great Monologues from the EST Marathon
The Great Monologues from the Women's Project
The Great Monologues from the Mark Taper Forum

YOUNG ACTORS SERIES
Great Scenes and Monologues for Children
New Plays from A.C.T.'s Young Conservatory
Great Scenes for Young Actors from the Stage
Great Monologues for Young Actors
Multicultural Monologues for Young Actors
Multicultural Scenes for Young Actors

SCENE STUDY SERIES
Scenes From Classic Plays 468 B.C. to 1960 A.D.
The Best Stage Scenes of 1993
The Best Stage Scenes of 1992
The Best Stage Scenes for Men / Women from the 1980's

CONTEMPORARY PLAYWRIGHTS SERIES
Romulus Linney: 17 Short Plays
Eric Overmyer: Collected Plays
Lanford Wilson: 21 Short Plays
William Mastrosimone: Collected Plays
Horton Foote: 4 New Plays
Israel Horovitz: 16 Short Plays
Terrence McNally: 15 Short Plays
Humana Festival '93: The Complete Plays
Humana Festival '94: The Complete Plays
Women Playwrights: The Best Plays of 1992
Women Playwrights: The Best Plays of 1993

CAREER DEVELOPMENT SERIES
The Job Book: 100 Acting Jobs for Actors
How to Audition for the Musical Theatre
The Camera Smart Actor
The Sanford Meisner Approach
The Actor's Chekhov
Kiss and Tell: Restoration Scenes, Monologues, & History
Cold Readings: Some Do's and Don'ts for Actors at Auditions

If you require pre-publication information about upcoming Smith and Kraus books, you may receive our semi-annual catalogue, free of charge, by sending your name and address to *Smith and Kraus Catalogue, P.O. Box 127, One Main Street, Lyme, NH 03768. Or call us at (800) 895-4331, fax (603) 795-4427.*

The Best
Men's Stage Monologues
# of 1992

Edited by
Jocelyn A. Beard

The Monologue Audition Series

SK
A Smith and Kraus Book

A Smith and Kraus Book
Published by Smith and Kraus, Inc.

Cover and Text Design by Julia Hill
Manufactured in the United States of America

First Edition: March 1993
9 8 7 6 5 4 3 2 1

Publisher's Cataloging in Publication
(Prepared by Quality Books Inc.)

The Best Men's Stage Monologues of 1992/edited by Jocelyn A. Beard
-- 1st edition
     p. cm.
     Includes bibliographical references.
     ISBN 1-880399-11-3
     ISSN 1067-134X

     1. Acting. 2. Monologues. I. Beard, Jocelyn A. II Title:
Best Men's Stage Monologues of nineteen ninety-two.

PN2080.B4 1993   792'.028
                                  QBI92-20371

Smith and Kraus, Inc.
One Main Street, PO Box 127, Lyme, New Hampshire 03768
(800) 895-4331

Acknowledgments

Grateful thanks to the playwrights and their agents.

Jocelyn A. Beard would also like to thank

Kevin Kitowski for his love and support.

Preface

What a season! With shows like *Dancing at Lughnasa,* and *Two Shakespearean Actors* gracing our stages this year, it's no wonder that our annual collection of monologue material is brimming with wonderful selections for men. In a year overshadowed by politics, it is particularly inspiring that men's roles in theatre have grown in scope and complexity without hindrance from the socio-political factors found daily in our national op-ed pages.

The men of the 1992 theatrical season can be found struggling to make ends meet in contemporary Ireland, battling a fever in an unknown time and place and in, perhaps, the most dangerous of all locations: the dreaded Fire Island vacation home of Terrence McNally's *Lips Together Teeth Apart.* Tackling life's challenges with courage and passion, the men found within these pages point us towards the future.

Playwrights like Wallace Shawn and Alan Ayckbourn have created men's characters in 1992 that stir, educate and provoke. 1992 gives us men fighting the ravages of alcoholism, men facing the inevitability of disease and death, men coping with the destruction of their country and men risking everything to discover new worlds. Happily, all is not dire. Plenty of comedic and downright silly characters have been included in the collection, rounding it out in a delightful manner.

Hopefully, you will find several pieces herein that will round out your own collection.

Break a leg!

Jocelyn A. Beard
Patterson, New York
Autumn 1992

Contents

Introduction

AH! The monologue! For years, we who labor in the vineyard of the theatre have hotly debated its status as the primary avenue on which we travel to meet new actors. Rage as it will, the debate has yielded no better solution.

Monologues are for the actor what a finely honed repertoire of pitches is for a major league pitcher. When you undertake "general" audition for a theatre, a casting director or an agent, you are "taking the mound" in a high stakes game. Your success depends on your mental and physical preparedness. YOU NEED TO BE READY. Further, you need to have a keen sense of the appropriate, of what is required. After five or ten minutes, you may begin a rich career, be asked into a company, secure a talent agent, or pass the first test towards winning the lead in the hot new American play of the season. Good fortune often begins with an intelligent selection and a keen rendering of one, or more monologues.

The actor often decries the lack of opportunity but then is not ready with a rich selection of audition pieces when opportunity knocks...and many auditions come your way with little notice, or time to prepare. In the early seventies a friend phoned me in a panic. "I've just been called by the casting office of the New York Shakespeare Festival to do a general audition for their season in the park...tomorrow!" "I'm not 'up' on two contrasting classical pieces! What do I do???" He crammed, he went, he faltered and stopped. The Actor's Nightmare.

You must know, that in the audition room we are *there* for you. We want you to WIN, we want YOU to be the person we are looking for. We are your strongest supporters and advocates! We want you to bring appropriate and arresting material. We want to be awakened to the uniqueness of YOU. Help us! Be smart about this task! Save the imaginative age leaps, the physical quirks and peculiarities and the richly detailed dialects for opportunities which specifically call for them. Dig and re-dig for current and intriguing material with which we might not be familiar. Choose works from productions which received important attention and which we might have not had an opportunity to see. Avoid the discontented winters of Richard III, the Queen Mab speech of Mercutio and Juliet's incantation to fiery footed steeds. Ask *not*, Joan, for the papal inquisition to "light your fires!"

The simple requirement in a general audition of two monologues; make choices of characters/pieces *in which you would be cast*. The choices, the selection of your audition material, not only tells us much about *you* as an artist (with, dare I say, specific sensibilities) but it is, as well, the most critical component of your homework.

This is a thrilling time in American playwriting. We are seeing fresh new voices and important new directions from established writers; all are responding to the world in which we live *today*. An itchy and challenging world, a world in search of profound relatedness, a world of rich possibility and opportunity! The monologues within these pages represent these voices and rich points of view. Many of them will not have been seen before as audition material. See this volume as the rich resource that it is. The editor has condensed an important piece of your homework… what an opportunity…seize it!

The great humanitarian, Thornton Wilder, characterizes actor's gift as a combination of three separate faculties or endowments: an observant and analyzing eye, the strength of imagination and memory, and arresting physical co-ordination…let me be presumptuous and add to that list…a dazzling array of pitches.

Finally, to every actor who is just beginning (be you 20 or 50) be unstoppable. Be who *you* are. Risk, dare, make the love choice and in the privileged calling to which we respond, find that in you which represents the highest actor power: YOUR HUMANITY.

Bruce Bouchard
Artistic Director, Capital Rep
Albany, New York

The Best
Men's Stage Monologues
of 1992

AFTER THE DANCING IN JERICHO
by P. J. Barry

Jim Conroy
After 30 years of friendship, Jim finally confesses to
conservative Kate that he's gay.

JIM: What's normal, Kate?

[**KATE**: Howard and I...our family...Yes! We all have....feelings but we don't have to act on them.]

[**GLORIA:** Ohhhh...]

[**KATE:** You and Gloria, too...you were a family...]

JIM: *(More riled.)* Yeah, we were, Kate. I wanted that with Gloria...wanted that normal life...and I was determined not to have those feelings. I would love her, I could love her, I did love her.

[**GLORIA:** Jim, don't go–]

JIM: *(Overlapping.)* But three days before we were married I was on the street and I saw a man and he caught my eye and then he passed and I stopped and turned around and he had stopped and was looking at me...it's called cruising, Kate...and then he started toward me and I panicked and moved away fast...full of fear...knowing I was attracted to him, aroused by him –

[**GLORIA:** Jim, this –]

JIM: Let me finish, Gloria. And three days later we were married and we were happy and it was steady going for a lot of years...normal...I managed to bury those feelings, but then with a few drinks, as time went on, the inhibitions would fade...torment disappear...let it rip! My double life began...loving husband and father and the other guy with the quick and sometimes sordid encounters. I loved it...hated it...full of good ole' Catholic guilt, full of shame...but I couldn't stop, didn't want to, normal out the window. So the double life went on and ate me alive...until I quit drinking and then I had to face more truth...not only an alcoholic...but gay, too.

...AND THE RAIN CAME TO MAYFIELD
by Jason Milligan

A gas station/luncheonette in Mississippi, 1962
Carl, a young photographer, 19
A young southerner with a photographic eye recalls his past.

CARL: You know, this is funny...but I was thinking before I came out here just now...how, when you remember something that happened a long time ago, it turns out to be just sort of a ghost of whatever it was that really happened. Details, even that you know you'll remember forever...grow fainter and fainter as years go by. *(Beat; he gestures to his camera.)* You can document the way things look – the way light filters through a windowpane, the lines in someone's face, whatever...but what you felt, thought, dreamed of...memory changes those intangibles into whatever it wants to. *(Beat; he regards the set.)* It doesn't matter, I don't guess. But there are some things I ought to tell you before all this starts. *(Carl crosses to center stage; lights on the set come up a bit but Emma and Mavis remain frozen.)* This is where I grew up: Mayfield, Mississippi. It's a combination luncheonette and gas station. Dad thought it'd be a great idea. He got a tip from one of those guys he went drinking with that they were gonna build I-55 down along State Highway 31, so he put his place up, hoping to make a killing off the Interstate traffic. But, as with everything Dad did, fate bypassed him. The Interstate was run south all right, but about twenty miles west of here. *(Beat.)* I imagine I sound sort of harsh when I talk about Dad, but again, that's how it is when you remember something. I probably eliminate a lot of his good qualities when I look back on him, but that's just it: memory distorts truth. No matter how close you try to stick to it. Like my whole meeting with Nathan, I have a picture of him; I know what he looked like...but what did we talk about? We probably said two or three words to each other, but in my mind, it was bigger – larger than life – actually sort of magical, cause it changed my life. Or, sparked a series of ideas that changed my life. *(Beat.)* I should probably just shut up and let this whole thing start. Let me just reiterate that this is where I grew up...in the Southern part of Mississippi. It's 1962. September. A really hot day in September. *(Suddenly becomes conscious of his eye.)* You'll hear more about my black eye, soon enough, so if you're wondering about that, just – you know – try to be patient. *(Looks at a small brown bag he carries.)* Oh, and I'm at the hardware store right now buying a new electric switch for that fan over there on the table. *(Starts to go, stops, smiles a charming smile.)* Hold still. *(He takes a picture of the audience.)*

ANOTHER TIME
by Ronald Harwood

Recording studio in London, 1985
Leonard, a concert pianist, 51
Leonard is a great concert pianist who has recently decided not to
perform in his native South Africa. When his son questions his motives, he
offers the following explanation.

LEONARD: Jeremy, please don't talk of things you know absolutely nothing about. When I first played the piano –
[**ROSE:** In my flat, above the library, a Mozart minuet, I remember it as if it were yesterday, he was five years old –]
LEONARD: Yes, I was five years old. I just went to the piano and played. Gran didn't arrange for me to have lessons in the hope that I'd have talent. The talent came first, and she arranged for lessons as a result. Talent has always been the taskmaster, and, yes, I don't deny, in certain respects, it came easily to me. At nine years old I sight-read the Beethoven C minor piano concerto. But it wasn't just a sight-reading, it was a "performance," as though I'd worked on the piece for months. And everyone marvelled, and I couldn't understand why because it was as natural to me as drawing breath. And it still comes naturally to me, yet why is it I have to practice and that some times I play sublimely and others like a blacksmith? On the good days I don't suddenly develop extra fingers or muscles, I don't have bionic arms or a computerized nervous system. So why is it that sometimes I have to struggle and fight and, yes, Mom, hammer the keys until the sweat pours down my face and back? Why? What's the problem, what's the secret? The problem is that the world impinges. When you're nine years old, or on the good days, you and the world are one, or there is no world, or there's just your world. The truth is, I can only play really well when the chasm between who I am and what I do disappears. That's why I practice. I practice to make the piece I play easy so that my physical actions are secondary to everything else. That's how it is. What I am is how I play. What I am and how I play are the reasons I won't go back. Yes, because talent is the taskmaster and talent has to be nurtured, protected, honed. And if

that means keeping the world at bay because I daren't risk any disturbance, so be it. And if my motives seem questionable and my means facile, if it seems easy to you, or cruel, then there is nothing more I can say. Yes, I'm willing to admit that the politics may be secondary because I have enough problems trying to play the piano, to invest the music I make with all the—all the—yes, and I enjoy cigars and champagne and parties and restaurants because I need to be with people, and because most of my life I spend alone at a piano, or in foreign hotel rooms, after a concert, watching television programs in languages I don't understand. And I play Rachmaninoff, Jeremy, because his soulfulness puts me directly in touch with my own emotions, aspirations, doubts, insecurities, innermost feelings. And I require that, like a drug. Because what I am is how I play.

ASCENSION DAY
by Michael Henry Brown

Virginia, 1831
Nat Turner, a slave on the verge of rebellion,
Afro-American, 30
The voice of God has instructed Nat to lead a rebellion on the
Virginia plantation where his people have labored and suffered.
On the eve of the insurrection, Nat prays a final time to God.

NAT: Lord...I be ready...I gots good men, Lord. I jest gots one...
one...nevah min'...I be ready. *(He wipes sweat from his brow.
Then he collapses on his stomach.)*

Ise prepared to do what evah it takes...Ise flesh an' blood...I knows
dis here be de moment you birthed me fo'. I know...but Ise an
ungrateful fool who loves life too much. Strike me dead now if I
be a coward on dis night...Ida been a strong angel, Lord. But dis
here...*(Nat laughs.)*

Dey all thinks I'm brave, but we know better don't we, Lord? Dey
thinks I will wave my hand an' smite dese white folks...But we
both know dat I don't wanna die an' I don't wanna kill
nobody...*(He rises back to his knees.)*

Why you gots to talk to me, Lord? Why you gots to make me so
smart, damn it! I coulda been stupid an' happy kissin' Massa's
ass...See, see, it yo' fault, Lord, you made me too bright not to be
'fraid. *(By now he is crying.)*

On dis here mornin' I am yo Angel o' Death...jest gimme de
strength o' life.

BEGGARS IN THE HOUSE OF PLENTY
by John Patrick Shanley

The dusty basement of a home in the Bronx
Pop, a bitter patriarch, 45-60
When his attitudes are challenged by his son, this angry man
reveals his contempt for his family.

POP: I don't know where ta start with you. My children? This is why I shouldn't feel alone? My children, my kids, the fountainhead of my dick, the little ones. But how they do grow! They'd a cut their teeth on my liver if it was put to 'em! They'd grab the sun outta the sky and stash it if they could! Cold comfort in their shade I shall not take. No, thank you. Or should I look to my brothers? My brothers are dead. Do you remember how I shook when they died, one after the other? And I hadda stand there in the suit, them stretched out inna box? While your aunts made jokes and dabbed at their crocodile tears, their heads full of insurance! Where's the soft shoulder for this old man in that? *(Spits.)* I'd rather suck onna stone. Or should I scavenge all the way back to Ireland, searching for something green? My father and mother, always in the middle of a fight. I'd come in. A pail of water'd fly by my face! Whoosh! Or a stool. Yeah! He made furniture and she'd say, "You can hide a lot with putty and paint." If she had been my wife! *(Gestures he would have struck her.)* He couldn't get along with anybody. Except me. Even the animals would run away from him. I had a family. And I outwitted them all, Johnny Lad, and you will, too, or you won't. Your mother...*(Joey cries a little and Pop is right on him.)* Was that a whimper? Whimper again and I'll whack you one!

BEGGARS IN THE HOUSE OF PLENTY
by John Patrick Shanley

The dusty basement of a home in the Bronx
Johnny, an Irish-American searching for love, 20s
Following a childhood devoid of love and acceptance, John finally
confronts his father with his failure.

JOHN: What's the matter with you? What's the matter with your soul? For Chrissakes, we coulda helped each other, Pop. The world is hard enough. Ain't it? Without no haven at all? I look like The Bronx inside. I could vomit up a burning car. You seen them. These dead wrecks everywhere. They've been abandoned. I feel them inside! And I was the lucky one! I was the fortunate son. What have you done to me? What did you do to your boys?

[**POP:** John.]

JOHN: No. Fuck you. You know what I feel when I see a beggar on the street? I wanna kick in his face! I wanna beat him ta death! Cause that's me! Pathetically waitin' with my fuckin' cup. But that's over. I've stopped stealin' and I've stopped settin' fires and I've stopped breakin' windows. And now, now I'm gonna stop waitin' for you. To reach down to me. To touch my face. To kiss my wounds. There's been a kinda silence fallen between us like a long drop onta sharp rocks. For a long time now. It's been my wait. I've been waitin' for something. Words, I guess. Some words. Do I have the words even now? *(Pause.)* I will never think of you without being shocked by your lovelessness. I will never think of you without a gasp of wonder. I will never think of you without some pain. And despite everything, in the face of everything, though it personally shames me to say it, I still have love for you.

8

BLACK SNOW
by Keith Dewhurst

A flat in Moscow, 1924
Maksudov, a struggling writer, male, 20s-30s
After receiving several rejection letters for his novel,
Maksudov contemplates suicide

MAKSUDOV: Well: my miserable life is ended. Why wouldn't the light bulb blow? *(Maksudov lights the kerosene lamp on the floor. Then he takes the Browning Automatic from his pocket and puts it down. He writes a note.)* I, Sergey Leontyevich Maksudov, hereby declare that I have stolen Browning Automatic number...from my friend Parfen Ivanovich...of number...Samotechnaya-Sadovaya Street, Moscow...who by the nature of his occupation has the right to carry a gun. What else? Nothing. Simply put the muzzle to my temple and pull the trigger...*(Maksudov puts the gun to his temple. His hand shakes.)* I am in mortal fear. Nevertheless...*(He feels for the trigger.)* The man starts to run through the room. There is a shot. With a groan the man falls headlong. He lies motionless and from his head trickles a black puddle. In the same sad dream I saw my native city, the snow, the winter, the Civil War...A snowstorm blew into my eyes and there was a grand piano. People stood 'round it. I was crushed by loneliness. I was afraid of death and awoke in tears. "It's an onslaught of neurasthenia," I said to the cat. "But don't worry, I won't die yet." So I began to write a novel. I described the snowstorm, and the cat liked to sit on the manuscript. I had my job reading proofs on the "Steamship Herald" but whenever I could I pretended to be ill and stayed home. I waited for the night. Only then was it quiet. I secluded myself. I lost my few acquaintances...But I did shave every day, and one night I raised my head and was amazed to see daylight. I realized that I had finished. I wrote "THE END" in big letters... Then I checked my novel from the point of view of whether it would...well...get past the censor. It became clear that it would not. Every line shouted that out. Having corrected it, I spent my last remaining cash on having two extracts copied, and took them to the office of a literary journal. A fortnight later I got them back. In the corner of the manuscript was written: "Not suitable." After cutting out this pronouncement with nail scissors, I took the same extracts to another literary journal and a fortnight later I got them back with precisely the same inscription: "Not suitable." Then the cat stopped eating...She huddled up in a corner, and drove me to distraction with her miaowing. This went on for three days. On the fourth, I found her dead on her side in the corner. I borrowed a shovel from the porter, and buried her in some waste ground...I'm utterly alone in the world but, frankly, in my heart of hearts, I'm glad. What a burden the unfortunate creature was...The autumn rains have arrived. Insomnia takes its toll. My shoulder aches, and my left knee. Work all my life on the "Steamship Herald"? Don't joke! Try to write another novel? Why? I've no message for mankind...*(Then a gramophone starts up in the flat below.)* My godfathers! Gounod's "Faust"! That really is on cue. *(An idea strikes him.)* I'll just wait for Mephistopheles' entrance. For the last time. Then I'll never hear it again. *(He realizes that the music is building to a climax.)* He's coming! Mephistopheles!

BLUE STARS
by Stuart Spencer

A suburban home, the 1950s
Freddy, a driver for a taxi company, 20-30
Here, Freddy tells a woman he called for by mistake about his
experiences flying planes in the Pacific during the war.

FREDDY: I could lose my job, ma'am. I told them I'd be here when they call. Please try to understand. I need this job. It was the only thing I could get, the only thing I've been able to hold onto. And there's competition for this kind of job, believe it or not. They'd fire me in a second if they had any trouble with me. They've told me so. There's plenty more where I came from—that's what they say. I'm not what you'd call highly employable. About the only thing I know how to do is fly a plane and they won't let me do that anymore on account of my injury. I caught some flak on the left side here and I haven't got any strength on my whole left side, see? So I can't fly. But I can drive all right. It's not the same, but sometimes I use my imagination and it almost seems like I'm flying again. That's why I need this job—it keeps me from going nuts. See, with any other job, it'd be impossible to even use my imagination; but driving the car, see, I pretend like it's my plane. My old plane. That old Ford out there. In my mind, while I'm tooling down East Main with the sunlight coming through the trees, I imagine I'm back in my little baby. Corsair. Best damn flying machine they ever built. And the treetops, the branches hanging down covered in leaves, they're the clouds. With the sunlight flickering through them. And the sky over me. And if I squint a little bit, I can imagine it's the whole earth below me, not just Main Street. *(Looks out the window.)*

You'd never think, looking at that old Ford, that anybody could use their imagination and make it into the best little fighter plane they ever saw. But I've got a powerful imagination. That's one thing about me—ever since I was a kid, I had a powerful imagination. I never lost it.

BRAVO, CARUSO!

by William Luce

Caruso's dressing room in the Metropolitan Opera House
Christmas Eve, 1920
Enrico Caruso, the great tenor, 40-50
While awaiting the evening's performance, Caruso entertains reporters in
his dressing room. Here, he talks about his family.

CARUSO: *(To picture.)* Mamma mia, what is happening to your little divo? You remember, that is what you call me. "Il mio piccolo divo, my little Carusiello."

(To reporters.) Mamma lose several babies. How many, she never tell. My brother Giovanni say I am number eighteen out of twenty-one. All the others die before me and one after. Twenty boy and one girl, he say. Maybe so, maybe no. Is a lotta babies.

Across the hall a neighbor have twenty girl and one boy. Just opposite. That's forty-two babies. Mamas and papas, that's forty-six. Eight grandparents, fifty-four. Fifty-four people in four rooms. And that's not counting the chickens. Well, that's Napoli.

How many of your wife give birth to twenty son? *(Pause.)* No? How about twenty daughter? *(Pause.)* You see? Is very unusual.

I was born on twenty-five day of February, year 1873, in Napoli. My father was name of Marcellino Caruso. A janitor. Mamma was Anna. She went without shoe, so that her Carusiello could study voice. Five lire every month she pay. She cut my shirt front of clean white paper, when I go to sing in church. When a little boy, lying in bed with the cover pull over my head, I remember Mamma and Papa argue violent over my future. Papa he say I gotta go work, be a mechanic. Mamma she want me to study, to sing. Mamma win the fight.

BRAVO, CARUSO!
by William Luce

Caruso's dressing room in the Metropolitan Opera House
Christmas Eve, 1920
Enrico Caruso, the great tenor, 40-50
While awaiting the evening's performance, Caruso entertains reporters in
his dressing room. Here, he talks about his beloved mother's death.

CARUSO: I have the benediction of Mamma till I was fifteen year.
During the Festival of Corpus Domini, she took ill, and I had to
sing at the Church of San Severino. *(To picture.)* I didn't want to
leave you, Mamma, even for an hour. But you order me to go. *(To
reporters.)* I was the chief boy contralto in Napoli, and Mamma
was very religious. She was just fifty year old three days before. So,
there I was, singing to the Blessed Virgin, and tell myself that
Mamma will be alive when I return home. In the middle of the
service, the neighbors come to tell me Mamma is gone. While I am
singing, her soul take flight. *(To picture.)* Mamma. Blessed
Mamma. Like the Madonna you are. I look at your face when I am
in a moment of discouragement, and I draw from it eternal
sympathy. *(To reporters.)* I wonder, where do such saints go at
death? It could not be too far. Do you know, honored gentlemen
of the press? Have you wondered, too? *(Touching heart.)* Maybe
in here. Si, I think so. En fondo o core. I feel her so close at times.
Do you have such feelings for those you lose? It is like a veil
between two worlds. So thin, so fragile. And sometimes, I think I
can pull it aside, reach out and almost touch that face, can almost
hear that beloved voice again. (To *Mamma, whispering.)* Mamma?
Mamma, I am here. Your little divo. Mamma, parlateme. For you is
all this, my work and my striving. You give me the gift of music. A
bright gift – in here. Music in my life is like wings to the bird. I sing
because I can do no other, ever since I was Carusiello, the little
one. Emotionated I become, emotionated and happy for joy.
Music is my paradiso. When I sing, I forget where I am, who I am. I
need music like water when I am thirsty. Mamma, parlateme. *(To
reporters.)* But then, she is gone. It is, after all, only a dream.

CAPTIVE
by Jan Buttram

Rural Texas, 1983
Gordon Pound, a crusty old man, 83
Gordon's wife may have been kidnapped by Shiite terrorists while on a
church-sponsored trip to the Holy Land. As he and his daughter anxiously
await word from the state department, he bemoans his age and physical
deterioration.

GORDON: If you don't help me do something, I don't know what…to find out about that little gal of mine, I may as well walk off into the Covington bottoms.

[**SALLY:** Couldn't sleep?]

GORDON: Hell, no. Can't sleep, can't eat, can't walk, can't do nothing. I sit up half the night. After fifty-two years of sleeping in the same bed, Maude won't sleep with me no more. She says I wrap myself up in the blanket and she near sweats herself sick. Well, I get cold. (*Pause.*) Maude sits staring out that kitchen window, she says she's waiting for that big crane that lives on the pool to fly off, but I know she's waiting for me to go on and die so she can fly off. She sees them other widow women getting around without any trouble.

[**SALLY:** C'mon now, Dad.]

GORDON: My body is giving way. I'm a hindrance to everybody. I can't keep cows anymore because I can't walk my own fence row. The only thing I could plant would be turnips because you just broadcast the seeds but I couldn't bend down to pick them once they was growed.

[**SALLY:** That's not true.]

GORDON: The devil it's not. You just don't know. You're never around here. Day before yesterday, I went out to saddle up Peanuts and take her for a ride on her birthday. She was twenty-one – near as old as me. That dagblasted pony stepped on my foot while I was saddling her up and I let out a good yell. She spooked and sided me up against the barn and I was trapped, by God. Couldn't move. I shoved and pushed and knocked and beat on that horse for ten minutes, but I didn't have the strength to get out from her. Clay rescued me after a spell. My foot had swelled up so bad, had to cut my boot off. *(Pause.)* Not two hours later, Peanuts dropped dead in the pasture. I believe that pony died of shame for not having the sense to move off my foot.

CEMENTVILLE
by Jane Martin

The locker room of a boxing arena in
Cementville, TN, the present
Kid, a boxer with a world view, 70
During the backstage confusion during a riot at a women's wrestling
event, Kid shoots Bigman, an obnoxious manager. As Kid prepares to exit
the locker room via a secret door to avoid the angry crowd, he tells
Bigman of his boxing heyday.

KID: Hurtin' people, now that's a serious gig, see. I don't play with
it. I don't fool nobody. *(Big smile.)* When I hurt 'em, I hurts 'em.
(Puts the cigarette in Bigman's mouth.) I ever tell you I fought
Sandy Sadler three times? Second fight a woman come to the
dressing room, bare shoulders, ball gown, took off a diamond
bracelet, give it to me, she said, "You, sir, gave a fine account of
yourself." *(He tips over a bank of lockers, stage right. Points at a
door behind the locker which has been revealed.)* Come right
through here in that China silk dress. Took me to her home on a
bluff overlooked a wide turn in the Mississippi and there we
danced the Samba to a sixteen-piece all-girl orchestra from
Venezuela. Sandy Sadler, he was there. Two-Ton Tony Galento, he
was in town. Ooooo, he was light on his feet. The referee, he
danced with the Governor's wife and a Secret Service man. Ol'
Jake Lamotta, he slow danced with a nine-year-old girl standin' on
his shoes. Oh, that was a sight. The waiters in their white coats,
they joined in. All of us laughin', hummin' along, all doing the
rumba, while the moon went down. *(He heads out.)* There was a
girl playin' clarinet in that band later left a camellia on my pillow.
(His voice recedes down the hall.) 'Course those were different
times. Different times. Different times.

DANCING AT LUGHNASA
by Brian Friel

The home of the Mundy family, Ballebeg, County
Donegal, Ireland, 1936
Jack, a missionary priest, 53
Malaria has forced Jack to return to Ireland from Uganda. As he recovers
from his disease in the home of his sisters, he shares some of his
missionary experiences.

JACK: What Okawa does – you know Okawa, don't you?

[**MAGGIE:** Your house boy?]

JACK: My friend – my mentor – my counselor – and yes, my house
boy as well; anyhow, Okawa summons our people by striking a
huge iron gong. Did you hear that wedding bell this morning,
Kate?

[**KATE:** Yes.]

JACK: Well, Okawa's gong would carry four times as far as that.
But if it's one of the bigger ceremonies, he'll spend a whole day
going 'round all the neighboring villages, blowing on this
enormous flute he made himself

[**MAGGIE:** And they all meet in your church?]

JACK: When I had a church. Now we gather in the common in the
middle of the village. If it's an important ceremony, you would
have up to three or four hundred people.

[**KATE:** All gathered together for Mass?]

JACK: Maybe. Or maybe to offer sacrifice to Obi, our Great
Goddess of the Earth, so that the crops will flourish. Or maybe to
get in touch with our departed fathers for their advice and
wisdom. Or maybe to thank the spirits of our tribe if they have
been good to us; or to appease them if they're angry. I complain
to Okawa that our calendar of ceremonies gets fuller every year.
Now at this time of year over there – at the Ugandan harvest time
– we have two very wonderful ceremonies: the Festival of the New
Yam and the Festival of the Sweet Casava; and they're both

dedicated to our Great Goddess, Obi –

[**KATE:** But these aren't Christian ceremonies, Jack, are they?]

JACK: Oh, no. The Ryangans have always been faithful to their own beliefs – like these two Festivals I'm telling you about; and they are very special, really magnificent ceremonies. I haven't described those two Festivals to you before, have I?

[**KATE:** Not to me.]

JACK: Well, they begin very formally, very solemnly with the ritual sacrifice of a fowl or a goat or a calf down at the bank of the river. Then the ceremonial cutting and anointing of the first yams and the first casava; and we pass these 'round in huge wooden bowls. Then the incantation – a chant, really – that expresses our gratitude and that also acts as a rhythm or percussion for the ritual dance. And then, when the thanksgiving is over, the dance continues. And the interesting thing is that it grows naturally into a secular celebration; so that almost imperceptibly the religious ceremony ends and the community celebration takes over. And that part of the ceremony is a real spectacle. We light fires 'round the periphery of the circle; and we paint our faces with coloured powders; and we sing local songs; and we drink palm wine. And then we dance – and dance – and dance – children, men, women, most of them lepers, many of them with misshapen limbs, with missing limbs – dancing, believe it or not, for days on end! It is the most wonderful sight you have ever seen! *(Laughs.)* That palm wine! They dole it out in horns! You lose all sense of time…!

Oh, yes, the Ryangans are a remarkable people: there is no distinction between the religious and the secular in their culture. And of course their capacity for fun, for laughing, for practical jokes – they've such open hearts! In some respects, they're not unlike us. You'd love them, Maggie. You should come back with me!

How did I get into all that? You must stop me telling these long stories. Exercise time! I'll be back in ten minutes; and only last week it took me half an hour to do number four. You've done a great job with me, Kate. So please do keep nagging at me.

DARK SUN
by Lisette Lecat Ross

A house in the poorer section of Soweto, South Africa, 1988
Simon Kgoathe, a black South African
victimized by the racist white government, 40s
When several Red Cross buses are attacked in the township of Soweto,
Simon manages to save Lydia, a white woman, from the violent mob. As
they hide from the police and the army in Simon's house, he tells Lydia of
the murder of his brother.

SIMON: *(With some bitterness.)* You want to know my earliest memory? My father. He worked on a farm. I remember this big white man screaming at him – "You *blerrie kaffir!* You big *blerrie* stupid baboon!" And my father, standing, with his hat in his hand and his head down, nodding, "Ja, my baas, sorry, my baas. Ja Basie. Ja Basie." My father knew I was looking at him. Afterwards, he couldn't speak to me. *(Pause.)* Then, one day, my son looked at me the same way! Oh, this system gives you so many things to be ashamed of... *(Bursts out, in pain.)* I would have gone for Lucas! I would have gone for him! Do you know how you feel when you hear it. Like someone has kicked you in your heart. You don't know what to do with the pain. It burns like a veldfire. I had many bad, bad dreams. I couldn't be around white people anymore. I left my job. I went to work in the cemetery. Oh, it made me feel good to look at all those dead *white* people. And when a new one came, I was so glad. When I cleaned 'round their stones, I would talk to them. Especially to one: "Andries Cronje – Dearly beloved husband – and father of Piet, Koos and Tinkie." He's got the same name as a prison warder at Leeuwkop. I hope it's him because I told him a lot of things. Heh! You can't believe how many good white people used to live in South Africa. All "kind" and "loving," all "dearly missed!" *(He crosses to check stove.)* This country! You must never forget. Forgetting just makes it worse the next time. And there's always a next time. Every time you think you've got a new plan for your life, God or the system or the white man will choose you. *(Pause, bitterly.)* My brother, Danny, was chosen.

(*Shakes his head.*) Of all people. Danny! His whole life was about music. That's all he thought about…(*Pause.*) He worked in the cafeteria at the University and, at night, he played in a mixed band on the campus. One night, the police raided them. They said there were "drugs on the premises." Danny was gone for two days. When he came back, he was so different. He didn't want to go to work. He didn't want to see his friends. He didn't even want to play music. And he wouldn't talk about it. I only learned much later what had happened. *First,* they made him stand in a room by himself, for twenty-four hours – without moving; without closing his eyes; without going to the lavatory. *Then* they said, oh, sorry, it's all a mistake. They gave him cigarettes, food, something to drink. And a man came to talk to him. A man who knew everything about Danny's life. Danny said his blood ran cold… The man said he had a very special job for him. He showed him some documents in another name – and a bank account. The first payment was already there! Danny couldn't believe it! He told them, no, I'm the wrong person. I won't make a good spy, I don't know anybody to inform about. The man said, you must let us decide. There are a lot of spies at the University who thought exactly like you in the beginning. It's very easy. All you have to do is let us know about any conversation, opinion, rumour, any small thing. Go home and think about it. Think of all the good things that will happen if you take the job. And the bad things that can happen if you don't. (*Pause.*) The very next morning they went to the house where his mother-in-law was working, illegally, and they took her away. (*Lydia is sitting immobile, listening intently.*) When you are chosen like this, your choices become too hard. (*Pause.*) But nobody knew. We just saw Danny was not the same happy-go-lucky person. Then, he disappeared again and when he reappeared, after three days, he looked very bad. That night he told me everything. He said he had given the police some false, useless information. They pretended to believe him. The man said, you've done good work but obviously your new friends don't trust you or they would have given you better information. You must be more enterprising. We will help you to give the right impression. They punched him and kicked him and beat him up. (*Pause.*) We talked a lot that night. I said he must tell his friends the truth. He screamed at me. He told me I was mad. Who would believe him. Everyone knows how cunning the security police are. You can't know the truth about anybody. He said he thought maybe he could be a double agent. But he didn't know how. And he was scared that anyone he spoke to might be a spy himself. *(Pause.)* That's when I started the cubbyhole. *(Pause.)* Later, the police arrested a woman from the University. They said they had "special information." They wouldn't say who supplied it but her friends said, from what the police "let slip," they knew it had to be Danny. He's the informer. And look how strangely he's behaving. He's guilty. Of course he's guilty. It's Danny.

DARK SUN
by Lisette Lecat Ross

A house in the poorer section of Soweto,
South Africa, 1988
Simon Kgoathe, a black South African victimized
by the racist white government, 40s
Here, Simon lashes out at the white government and their
systematic destruction of his people.

SIMON: They killed him. The people. They came at two o'clock in the morning, just like the police. He didn't have time to escape. His wife came to call me. I tried to explain. I told them the story. They said if I knew so much maybe I was involved. Maybe I was an informer, too. They didn't believe me. They didn't even want to listen. They tied his hands behind his back, they put a tire soaked in petrol around his neck and they set it on fire. *(Pause.)* *Magadlani* – "the joker." That's what they called him. Danny *Magadlani*. He could always make people laugh. *(Gazes out of the window.)* I didn't help anybody. I didn't help my son, I didn't help Danny. I didn't help Sipho.

[**LYDIA:** You helped me… *(She trails off, realizing the irony.)*]

SIMON: The first thing I will ask God is, "Why?" He better have a good explanation.

[**LYDIA**: *(Looks at the cross and chain in her hand. Impul-sively.)* Simon…? *(Crossing to him.)* Can I give you this? I want you to have it. Please. I'd like you to give it to your wife. *(She presses it into his hand.)* Please! Please take it. *(Reluctantly, Simon takes it. Somewhat stunned but nonetheless pleased with what she's done, Lydia settles down on the bed.)*]

SIMON: *(Slowly, as his fingers absently play with the cross and chain.)* Do you know the worst thing the white man does? It's not to keep the land for himself; to make us exiles in our own country; it's not that we work to keep him rich and comfortable – while he keeps us poor; it's not even that he took away our right to say *where* we live, *who* we marry, what kind of work we do; to vote... *(He pauses. She stretches, trying to ease her stiffened joints then, pulling the blanket around her, she gets into a more comfortable position. Simon is lost in thought. Only a seeming digression.)* When I was in prison, after a while, my brain began to feel totally dry – useless – like an old shrivelled up jacaranda seed. even your memories get worn out. One of the warders – Jan de Wet – I remember. He gave me a book. He saved my life. It was not even a very good book but it was like water to my dehydrated brain. Oh! I was so grateful! For one little book! *(Crosses to sit opposite her.)* It's what the first man wanted – out of the whole Garden of Eden! The tree of knowledge! A man has to know. He wants to learn; to find out things; to understand. Lucas deserved better. A *man* deserves better! Every man! He must grow. He must become more than he is! *(He leans forward.)* All you have at the end of your life is who you are. And who you are, it's what you know. And, *if* you go anywhere afterwards, that's what you'll take with you. That is all you take. That's you! Now, maybe you don't go anywhere! Ja! Maybe it's – *(Peers at her.)* Gah! What's the point! You are fast asleep.

THE DAYS OF WINE AND ROSES
by J.P. Miller

A meeting of Alcoholics Anonymous, 1960s
Joe Clay, an alcoholic struggling to cope
with his disease, 30-40
Following years of substance abuse, Joe is finally able to face his demons.
Here, he addresses the members of AA for the first time.

JOE: Thanks, Fred… My name is Joe, and – *(He clears his throat.)* – and I'm an alcoholic. *(He takes a deep breath and lets it out, relieved. Then he smiles broadly.)*

I've never said that in public before. I've said it to Fred, in private. But he's my sponsor, as you know, and I was in a straight-jacket at the time, and I thought that telling him that I was an alcoholic just like him, whether I meant it or not, was a nice way to thank him for putting cigarettes between my lips and lighting them for me. I also told my wife I'm an alcoholic, but she says I'm not, because I'm just like her and she's not. But that's another story… My mom and dad were a night club act – still are, somewhere – I'm not sure where at the moment. When I was a kid, everything they did had to do with booze. Get a booking? Celebrate. Meaning get drunk. Close a split week? Forget by getting drunk. Can't pay the rent? Get drunk and forget it. Have a birthday? Get drunk and laugh. A friend dies? Get drunk and cry. After the last show they always had a few to "relax." Not me. Too young. I had to relax by watching them get drunk. You can get pretty tense, believe me, relaxing that way.

Then, when I was fourteen, we were playing a small room in Vegas and bombing out and my mom entered a beautiful legs contest and won. They stuck a big sexy picture of her outside the lounge with "Mrs. Las Vegas Legs" emblazoned on it, and we started selling out and were held over. To help them celebrate, they let me have a drink – a nice icy stinger – my first drink ever. It was *delicious.* All I could think of was – how could I have wasted all those years? Well, I continued to celebrate my mom's election as Mrs. Las Vegas Legs from that day on with great enthusiasm. I didn't even notice when she had to start wearing slacks in the act to cover a permanently swollen knee, just kept right on celebrating. Somehow one day I found myself in a state which I mistakenly referred to as adulthood, and employed in a very sober business, where the workers never drink unless they're alone or with somebody – public relations. My way of doing business was to say, "Let's have a drink and talk it over." It's amazing how many people think that's a good idea. So I moved up in the world – good job, plenty of good friends to party with – almost everything, in fact, a man could want out of life. And then, to top it all off, I met Kirsten, and I did have it all. Kirsten was then, and is now –

(The lights dim to black as he speaks.)

– my great love, and the most wonderful person I've ever known.

DEJAVU
by *John Osborne*

A home in the Midlands, England, the present
J.P., a sardonic autocrat, 50+
Here, we discover the caustic J.P., who first appeared in
Osborne's "Look Back In Anger." 30 years later J.P. has grown
into his anger, which he now wears as a protective mantel. Here,
he takes on the local minister.

J.P.: You should read our parish magazine and see what's going on at England's heart.

[**HELENA:** Should I?]

J.P.: Its hard-hitting editor is none other than our fearless young abductor, the Rev. Ron. And here he is, on the front page, beside the Chancel Roof Appeal, featuring our very own axe-happy iconoclast, young James, as the subject of this month's "Ron Speaks with Christ" column. "I should have liked to take as my talking point young James Porter, a personal friend of mine and a popular figure in our Parish. However, Jim, as you all know, is at present in a spot of public bother, and I am unable to discuss his situation while the matter is *sub judice*. But it does allow me to bring to your attention the plight of similar young people all over our nation. Folk who are daily being driven to violence, acts of destruction and degradation, by evil forces and often through no fault of their own making. Take the widely reported case of Greville Plumb, a fourteen-year-old who ran away from home and family to hustle for a living in London, and was forced by sheer hunger to sell his only asset, his body, and was brutally, painfully, murdered. Either we push our young into the waiting arms of pimps and drug-pushers in the nearest metropolis, the criminal sub-culture that is lying in wait to exploit them; or we show them we need them, want them to stay and provide them with the prospect of a decent standard of living. To its credit the Church is showing at last that it really wants the young to be included in its life and worship. It is offering space for the young to meet (either in the church itself or in an annex to the Parish Room) – somewhere where they can play music, be themselves, and find their space. We should all give the PCC and the Parish Council every support in ending the cycle of deprivation and disenchantment to which the young have been subjected. NOW, before it's too late." That's telling 'em. Well, it's past remedy, I'd say, wouldn't you? I'd say yoof custody was preferable to chat-along-a-Ron. Rather face the spears of Captain Shanks's deadly dervish than the plain pop chat of that parson. In the face of such things, Madam, I have become very Saracen.

DOWN THE FLATS
by Tony Kavanagh

A flat in Dublin, the present
The Father, patriarch of a dysfunctional Irish family, 57
Following an evening out, the Flynns return home and prepare forbed.
Somewhat muddled by alcohol, The Father reminisces about singing, his
father-in-law and his job.

FATHER: I'll be in in a minute. *(He sits on the couch and starts to sing.)* "… I wish I was in Carrickfergus, only four nights in Ballygrand. I …" Ah, I'll never be the singer I was. I could sing a song and bring a tear to a woman's eye. But that was years ago, too many as a matter of fact. *(He turns and looks at the bedroom door and shouts.)* The only good laugh I had with your oul fella, Mary, was when we went out persecuting cats one night. *(He looks away from the door.)* How times go by. I sat there and watched it disappear, twenty-five years of me life, in that devil of a job, pickin' up other people's dirt, and me own son, the apple of her eye, turns out to be a litter bug… Christ almighty. Sure how am I to have respect for me job? *(Pause.)* I should of been many things but now I'm none of them. *(He falls off to sleep, mumbling under his breath. Then wakes again.)* My mother was a lady. She walked proud up the street, her head held high, and me poor father, like a fucken eegit, walkin' behind her. *(Pause.)* One day, one day … one day … God knows, one day. *(He falls into a deep sleep. He remains there for two minutes. Enter Mother in her nightdress. She stands and looks at him. She starts to shake him in order to wake him.)*

THE EARLY HOURS OF A REVILED MAN
by Howard Barker

A city street at night
Sleen, a novelist and doctor, 40-50
Following a day of treating the poor, whom he despises, this bitter man
walks the city streets and muses on the consistency of war.

(He walks the city. His stick taps.)

SLEEN: Some years ago I should have found a mistress. This would
have been my first recourse. *(A burst of intoxicated laughter. A
staggering of heels.)* And in her dishevelled room, all little bottles
and pulp of undistinguished poets, I should have lain with my eyes
on the ceiling rose, the conversation not flowing, the conversation
false, a cloud of compliments, etcetera, a cloud of flattery,
etcetera, not lucid, not limpid, but – *(The grinding of heels.)* Don't
knock into me, I am a war veteran! *(The stick continues.)* They
fling you over, they topple you, how easily toppled we are! And
rightly, since we have so presumptuously risen onto our hind legs.
no wonder we topple, of course the war was ecstasy, but who
dares say so now? *(He shouts.)*

THE EVIL DOERS
by Chris Hannan

Glasgow, the present
Tex, a philosophical loan shark, 20s
Here, Tex confronts the daughter of the man he has been trying
to bully money from. The loan shark has no choice left but to
resort to violence, which he clearly finds distasteful.

TEX: I question myself.

[**SUSAN:** Tex.]

TEX: I really begin to question myself. "What am I doing?" –
right? Am I trying to keep a family together? Because, fuck. See,
when people ask me what I do (gets on your tits right enough),
people ask me, I say: me? – something like the St. Vincent de Paul.
I visit the poor; and I like to remain anonymous. But you people! –
To give you another perspective: I'm watching you, right? The
whole family's surveying a piece of waste ground, twenty to
seven, no panic. Then scatter. All of a sudden scatter. Did
someone lob a grenade at you? Then I get 'round; and you're
stripping your father's one and only asset, then he comes after you–

[**TRACKY:** Is he still coming after me?]

TEX: – then he chucks it! (heads for, Christ, Ingram Street) and I'm
left here like that: family? – what family? – thin air. Then my car
breaks down. – Am I communicating right? Can I introduce
myself: I am not a social worker. – Fear. I say that, because no fear
– you're one emotion short. A normal family: they're all over the
place, chaos, then I go and see them. And they've got structure
then. So fine, so it's temporary – so is the universe. Even the solar
system isn't stable, could fly off the handle at any moment and
bastarding Jupiter: it's not even solid: volcanic gases or some
fuck'n'thing … (chaos). Normal family, I go in there and give them
a crisis and they're like that: they like it: because at least it's
something … takes their mind off their other problems.

EVIL LITTLE THOUGHTS
by Mark D. Kaufmann

A hitman's apartment, the present
Lloyd, a paranoid businessman, 40-50
When his business is threatened by a corporate raider, Lloyd hires a
hitman to eliminate the competition. When the hired killer asks
that they postpone the murder so that he may attend the
Ice Capades, Lloyd explodes.

LLOYD: We are not playing sandbox! We're not going to unroll our blankets and take a nap after cookies and milk! We're planning a murder!! Ice Capades?? What's wrong with you?

And this fucking Byzantine plot with winks and gestures, and this window, that sofa, three o'clock, five o'clock, and he's got a different identity, and who can even follow the damn thing??

In forty-eight hours we'll be in the apartment of a man I want dead, which you've known about for weeks. But you've put it off, and you haven't done your homework, and you've waited until today to throw this mish-mash of a plot together … So now we have to cram for the murder.

Walter told me you'd be the guy for the job. Serves me right to trust a man who has the same thing for lunch every day. Serves me right to trust a man who's got a hit man for a friend.

I mean, I heard talk. Rumors about how his wife died. I thought it was a joke. I was joking – almost joking – when I asked him where I could find a hit man. Who would have guessed he would have answered, "How much do you want to spend?" And that moment it was suddenly…so easy. Just hire someone to do it…like maid service. And there I was considering murder. And it was…exciting. I felt charged. Somehow my finger dialed your number – it had a life of its own…like automatic pilot… *(Lloyd examines his finger.)*

This finger used to hold little puppets in kindergarten. I mean little five-year-old Lloyd couldn't kill anybody. My God – what would I tell my mother?? "Hello, Mom? There's this really terrible man who wants to buy my business, and he won't take 'no' for an answer, so I've decided to kill him. What's so shocking? He's a bad person. He doesn't need my little paste company – he's got a glue empire. And a wife. Why should he have what's mine, too? It's not fair! Nuts! He needs to learn a lesson. He needs to be dead." What am I saying? I can't tell her that. What am I doing here? What happened to "Thou Shalt Not Kill"? I remember being told that was pretty basic stuff. Murder is not ethical under any circumstances – there's no hedging – that's it!! I am not going on with this business, so let's just forget about it...

THE FEVER
by Wallace Shawn

Here and now.
A delirious traveler, male or female, any age
A person traveling in a third world country is stricken with a
fever. He is confronted by the hostility of the masses towards
wealthy people.

TRAVELER: About a year ago I spent a day at a nude beach with a
group of people I didn't know that well. Lying out there, naked, in
the sun, there was a man who kept talking about "the ruling
class," "the elite," "the rich." All day long, "The rich are pigs,
they are all pigs, some day those pigs will get what they deserve,"
and things like that. He was a thin man with a large mustache,
unhealthy-looking but very handsome, a chain-smoker. As he
talked, he would laugh – sort of bitter barks that came out always
unexpectedly. I'd heard about these words and these phrases all of
my life, but I'd never met anyone who actually used them. I
thought it was quite entertaining. But for about a month
afterward a strange thing happened. Everywhere I went I started
getting into conversations with people I met – on a train, on a bus,
at parties, in the line for a movie – and everyone I met was talking
like him: The rich are pigs, their day will come, they're all pigs, and
on and on. I started to think that maybe I was crazy. I thought I
was insane. Could this really be happening? Was everyone now a
Communist but me?

FLAUBERT'S LATEST
by Peter Parnell

The garden of a country home in Western Connecticut,
mid-summer, the present
Gustave Flaubert, the novelist, 40-50
When a seance accidentally delivers Gustave Flaubert to a
weekend party in Connecticut, the misplaced novelist takes a
moment to share a bit of his philosophy with a contemporary fan.

GUSTAVE: What I am doing… What I am trying to do…is to find a language of the ordinary. To write about ordinary people, everyday life, but with a poetry that raises my characters' passions and thoughts to the level of myth, to the epic and the grand. Is this possible? If so, then I shall prove my two greatest beliefs: that, in literature, there are no beautiful subjects, only subjects written about beautifully; and that, therefore, no one subject is more important than any other. More duck? These morello cherries are superb! *(Pause.)*

All things must be raised to the highest level by the artist, who is a giant pump that reaches down into the deepest, darkest layers of things and shoots them up into the light. These heights can be achieved only through the slow and painful search for a proper style. And that style must exhibit its own reason for being, irrespective of its subject. It must possess the rhythm, the movement, the *feel* of verse, while still being prose? Wine? Yes, a little more, *un peu*… *(Pause.)*

Am I accomplishing such a style? *Peut-etre*, but only with the profoundest, most backbreaking labor. And only by *living* the very book that I am trying to write. I rise at noon, breakfast with maman or with Cicero, my *chien*. Read my mail, which almost always contains a letter from Louise, and give a grammar or history lesson to my niece Caroline. At two I go to my study. I sit at a large, round oak table, covered with a kind of netting so that the servants cannot try to tidy or neaten it up. In winter there is a fire going. In summer the windows are open. I wear a white silk dressing gown which reaches down to my feet. I place two blank pieces of paper in front of me, one beside the other. On the one on the right I begin to write, working quickly, freely, letting the thoughts and images flow, adding more pages as I go. After several pages, I return to the beginning, and start to rework, correct, word by word, sentence by sentence, line by line. There are soon so many changes, additions, deletions, that even I can barely read it. I then re-copy the page onto the blank page beside it. Then, and only then, I try to read aloud what I have so far written. The sentences must sound perfect. Forget about what they mean, though that, too, is important. They must possess a value as pure sound, the words must be absolutely the right words, expressing an idea perfectly expressed. By eight o'clock I stop, having perhaps rewritten, if I am lucky, half a page. Some days I only manage a single sentence. The more sentences I write, the more verbs and consonances, assonances and cacophonies conspire to drive me mad. Conjunctions make me sweat. Adjectives come to terrify me. Maman calls me to dinner and I am spent, utterly and completely, for an hour or two. Then I return to work, writing into the night. Again, if I am lucky, I lose myself until two or three. And after, when everyone else has long gone to sleep and I feel as if I am the only human left awake on the face of the earth, I write a long letter to Louise, sometimes in ecstasy, usually furious with myself for having worked so slowly and unsuccessfully.

(The lights around Gustave rise to include Felix, to whom he is addressing all this last. It is the same day, now night. A giant feast has taken place out in the garden, and Gustave is still eating. On the table are empty plates, glasses, and leftovers: a potage bonne femme, a mackerel, French beans, fried potatoes, a ricandeau of veal with sorrel, a roast duckling with cherries, apricot tart, three custards, a Mignon cheese, pears, plums, grapes, two bottles of Burgundy, a Chablis, and cake. The house is lit up, and there are candles and lights around the garden. The side table has been arranged with many more papers and books around it, which is where Felix is sitting.)

This does not change. None of this ever changes. Not for months and months and months. Three weeks ago I spent five days writing one page. I thought I was going to go mad. The words began to dance in front of me, to attack me in the middle of the night. Sentences rang in my head one way, then another. My friends urge me to come to Paris, to breathe the breath of life. But I hate their breath of life! I try to tell them it is not fame that interests me. If the work is good, it will attract its own fame. I must write for myself, because who else is there to write for? But can I ever please myself? Can I ever feel the work that I have done is good? How can I feel that when, day in and day out, the war to write words goes on, turning them, spitting them, eating them, farting them, kissing them, fucking them, killing them…with never a break, never a change, except maybe to stop and re-read someone else's greater work that only makes me feel like I am slipping down the mountain again…? No matter. When it sounds good, it is still the greatest feeling in the world. To move through an entire universe of one's own creation, to be man and woman, lover and mistress, the horse and the rider, the trees and the leaves and the road and the sun shining down upon it… To dream, to fail… What else is there?

FORTINBRAS

by Lee Blessing

The castle of Elsinore, Denmark, immediately following
the events of *Hamlet*
Polonius, an uphappy ghost, 50-60
Here, the ghost of Polonius describes his death to the audience.

(A castle hall. Polonius appears. He carries with him the Queen's old tapestry. He stops, looks around to make sure no one's there. Satisfied, he spreads out the tapestry, finds the hole made by Hamlet's sword.)

POLONIUS: *(Touching it.)* Here. *(Touching his chest.)* Here. *(To the audience.)* It does something to a man's point of view when he suddenly feels a sword go through his heart. I was pinned like a bug against the wall. Where was all my good advice then? Stuck in my throat, where it's remained ever since. Oh, I still have plenty of advice, don't misunderstand. I could tell everybody in this castle, living and dead, what to do. But to hell with 'em, that's what I say. *(Sighing.)* If there were a hell. There doesn't seem to be, for me. No heaven either, that I've been able to discern. Only this – wandering around the scene of all my errors, watching everyone make the same old mistakes, *burning* to advise them – and hating myself for it. Death has been my greatest disappointment. It's too much like life. I thought there would be a great adventure, but there's no great adventure. I've asked the King, the Queen, the others – no one's had a great adventure. So far, there's been nothing to compare with that first moment, pinned against a wall, translated by a steel point – my face buried against the blank side of a tapestry – hoping that in a single instant all might finally be revealed. *(Tossing over the corner of the tapestry.)* What a hoax. Death has all the uncertainty of life, and twice the solitude. If you take my advice – and no one ever does – you'll avoid it. *(Polonius turns to go. As he does, Fortinbras steps into view. Polonius freezes.)*

GORGO'S MOTHER
by Laurence Klavan

A park in Manhattan, the present
Brian, a snide but secretly emotional preppie, who
loves the movies, early 20s
Brian has been trying, unsuccessfully, to date Joanne. Here, he
tells her of his long-time love affair with the silver screen.

BRIAN: Oh, horror films are great. But not as great as James Bond – the early Connerys, of course, before they gave him a cartoon cock. And all those old musicals, Gene Kelly with that shoulder-to-shoulder smile. As a kid, I'd never seen anyone so – big before. That's what I wanted, never to be nervous, to feel so – enormous, you know? I used to dance around my room at home, trying to grow larger than life, my feet tapping on the floor, my head scraping the ceiling. I used to stay up late, moving from late show to late show, like I was crossing into different countries, searching for giants. *(Beat.)* My parents were opposed to my interest; they were sure I was going to be gay. They spent a long time learning to accept their gay son. And when it turned out that I wasn't, they didn't know what to make of me. It was like I had let them down. "But he watched so many movies," they said. They blamed themselves. My father thought, if only he had been weaker or more insensitive, or whatever the studies say. Even now, if I brought a girl home, I think they'd run from the room weeping. I think they wanted everything to be in order for me, for me to have a beginning, a middle and an end. I just think, in their own way, *they'd* been watching too many movies, too. *(Beat.)* Of course, I never have brought a girl home to them. Not yet. *(Beat.)* Next Friday, Joanne, it'll be *Gorgo* and *Mothra.*

I HATE HAMLET
by Paul Rudnick

A brownstone apartment in New York, the present
Andrew, a popular television star, 30s
When Andrew accepts the offer to perform Hamlet in a New
York production, he is visited by the ghost of John Barrymore,
who has been sent to help him prepare for the role. Here, Andrew
describes his performance to his phantom coach.

[**BARRYMORE:** But…you were ghastly. You said so. Dierdre agreed. The papers – everyone in New York.]

ANDREW: I heard. And that's part of it. Last night, right from the start, I knew I was bombing. I sounded big and phony, real thee and thou, and then I started rushing it: "Hi, what's new in Denmark?" I just could not connect. I couldn't get ahold of it. And while I'm…babbling, I look out, and there's this guy in the second row, a kid, like 16, obviously dragged there. And he's yawning and he's jiggling his legs and reading his program, and I just wanted to say, "Hey, kid, I'm with you, I can't stand this either!" But I couldn't do that, so I just kept feeling worse and worse, just drowning. And I thought, okay, all my questions are answered – I'm not Hamlet, I'm no actor, what am I doing here? And then I get to the soliloquy, the big job, I'm right in the headlights, and I just thought, oh Christ, the hell with it, just do it!
>   To be or not to be, that is the question;
>   Whether 'tis nobler in the mind to suffer
>   The slings and arrows of outrageous fortune,
>   Or to take arms against a sea of troubles
>   and by opposing, end them.

And I kept going, I finished the speech, and I look out, and there's the kid – and he's listening. The whole audience – complete silence, total focus. And I was Hamlet. And it lasted about ten more seconds, and then I was back in Hell. And I stayed there. But for that one little bit, for that one speech – I got it. I had it. *Hamlet*. And only eight thousand lines left to go.

JUDEVINE
by David Budbill

The landing of a logging operation somewhere in
Judevine, Vermont, late December, the present
Doug, a jack-of-all-trades; more restless than shiftless, 25-55
Among other vocations, Doug has pumped gas, trucked gravel
and farmed. Now he operates a crawler at a logging camp. Here,
he arrives for work and offers some early morning
philosophy to a co-worker.

DOUG: Couldn't drag myself outta bed.
My back is killin' me. That goddamn crawler
is about to do me in. Pinched a nerve or somethin',
Hurts like hell.
And this weather don't help neither.
I always thought that Conrad was a crazy stupid fool,
but maybe he ain't; maybe he knows what he's talkin' 'bout.
He was sayin' t'other day he thinks this ugly weather's 'cause
of all that walkin' on the moon or 'cause
that air pollution's eatin' holes into the sky. Hell,
you know it's worse than it ever used to be,
and the birds ain't actin' right.
Too goddamn cold too soon!
Why, this morning when I stepped outside to blink
my eyeball froze right open and my feet froze to my shoes!

[**ANTOINE:** Ah, Dougie.]

DOUG: It don't make it easy.

[**ANTOINE:** Dat be da Bible truth!]

DOUG: Well, there's only one thing worse than all this crazy
weather
and that's what's called the holy state of matrimony.

Holy, hell! It's like livin' with the devil!
You go out and get yourself a hen, she clucks around
for about a year or two, then she gets broody
and she begins ta cackle; you get too close that hen'll
peck ya. She'll sit around all day, watch them soaps
and all the time be eatin' up your money.
Christ, if I'da known I'da never done it.
It's a terrible price to pay for rollin' 'round the bed.
Jesus! how I wish I'd been smart like Tommy. Stay away
from the church and all that marryin' stuff. I wish I'd been
like him. Stop in at night, see his little lady, dip in
and go. That kid is free!
He ain't locked inside a hen house every night.
Hell, it's too late for me. I'm a domesticated cock,
and what's worse there's only one hen in my flock.
By Jesus, I'm a slave for life.
(To the audience.)
Listen boys out there, stay the fuck away from church.
Don't be like me and spend your life
wishin' you were someplace else and cryin'
to yourself 'bout how you didn't know how it would be.
Take it from me, she can catch you in a minute,
then she'll be done, but you'll have the chain
around your chicken leg for all your days!
You catch one and you think you've got
a sweet young thing, soft as a puffball on a tree.
You get her home and, mister, you have got a witch!
She'll change into a bully spruce so rough
it hurts to look. And ugly! Christ!
you just don't know. She'll drink your booze
and eat your food, get fatter than a sow.
She'll piss and moan and scream at you.
She'll belch and fart and lock you out!
Don't do it, boys! Don't you get caught!
By Jesus Christ, I wish to hell
I'd run until I'd lost her.

LA MAISON SUSPENDUE
by Michel Tremblay

A log cabin house at Duhamel, Quebec, the
present, and 1950
Jean-Marc, a man searching through his family's past, 48
When he purchases the house that served as his family's summer
home for several generations, Jean-Marc finds his thoughts
turning to their experiences there.

JEAN-MARC: Usually, when you buy a house, you say to yourself, "Ah, there are good vibes, here"... Sometimes it's true and sometimes it's only to convince yourself that you've made the right choice. *(He stands up.)* But, you see, when I came to look at this house in the spring, as soon as I walked in I knew this was the right place; that this house was waiting for me...it was the vibes of my own family that were for sale... I even bought it from my father's brother-in-law... In the hundred years that this house has stood, it's my own family that has fought here, argued here, made peace, cried, tapped its feet, played the fiddle and the accordeon, sung songs and made up new jigs. There have been unforgettable parties; crazy funerals; an especially odd marriage, quite sad actually, that turned my grandfather into my great uncle... My mother came here to get a break from me one summer, 'cause I'd just had scarlet fever and I was unbearable; ma tante Albertine and mon oncle Edouard tried to make peace, maybe right here on the verandah... My cousin Marcel played with his frigging imaginary cat... Ma tante Madeleine was dumped here by her husband, almost every summer of their lives, while he chased women all over the Province... All that belongs to me, Mathieu, it's all part of my heritage; in fact, it's my only heritage. I would have bought this house even if I'd been disappointed by it after all these years; even if the roof was caving in and the porch was rotten...even if it had been unliveable. I bought all those memories to keep them from sinking into indifference.

LIPS TOGETHER TEETH APART
by Terrence McNally

A beach house on Fire Island, the present
Sam, a man afraid of losing his wife, 30-40
Sam has discovered that his wife has been sleeping with his
sister's husband. A simplistic guy from New Jersey, Sam finds
that the task of coping with the fact of Sally's betrayal is tearing
him apart.

SAM: My brain has become a collision course of random thoughts. Some trivial, but some well worth the wonder. Sometimes I think I'm losing my mind. I'm not sure of anything anymore. It's the same anxiety I have when I think I've forgotten how to tie my tie or tie my shoelaces or I've forgotten how to swallow my food and I'm going to choke on it. Three days ago I was standing in front of our bathroom mirror in terror because I couldn't knot my tie. I wanted to say, "Sally, please come in here and help me." But I couldn't. What would she have thought? Last night I spit a piece of steak into my napkin rather than risk swallowing it, because I was afraid I would choke. Maybe it's trivial and that's why no one wants to talk about it, so I'm talking to myself. No one wants to listen to who we really are. Know somebody really. Know you leave shit stains in your underwear and pick your nose. Tell a woman you've forgotten how to swallow your food and she's in her car and out of your life before you can say, "Wait, there's more. Sometimes I have to think about someone else when I'm with you because I'm afraid I won't stay hard if I don't. Or how much I want to fuck the teenage daughter of the couple that lives three doors down. How my father takes all the air out of the room and I can't breathe when I'm with him. How if I could tear my breast open and rip out my heart and feed it to these sea gulls in little raw pieces, that pain would be nothing to the one I already feel, the pain of your betrayal! How most afraid I am of losing you." How can I tell you these things and there be love?

THE LITTLE TOMMY PARKER
CELEBRATED COLORED MINSTREL SHOW
by Carlyle Brown

A pullman car in a railroad yard, 1895
Tambo, an African-American minstrel, 50-60
As members of a minstrel show hunker down in a pullman car,
they share stories and memories of the past. Here, Tambo
remembers the story behind a particularly interesting song.

TAMBO: He wrote that song for a young girl out a Memphis, name a Rachel Green. I guess she was about nineteen. She was as black and shiny as your shoes, Henry. Like a black stone just out the sea. Like a raven, she was, black and pretty. The smoothest skin you ever saw. She had this way 'bout her, a cockin' her head and rollin' her big, black eyes up at ya, like she wasn't quite gettin' what you was sayin'. Them eyes could knock a man down. She was shapely too. Yeah, that girl had a fine body on her. If you could keep your eyes from lookin' into hers, you would see what a fine figure she had. Percy was doin' pretty good then. He was a feature singer and I was an endman with the Hall and Thompson's slave troupe, outa Albany. We was in Memphis. Percy sang this song he wrote, "De Darkies Dancin' Do." They loved it. It cracked everybody up. Everybody. Audience called him back three times. Three times. I guess you know what that does for your act after the show. When he looked into that gal's big black eyes, that was all there was to it. He was in love... She wanted him to make his mark in her program. Percy said, "Mark? Girl, I can sign my name, read and write both words and music. Sing and dance, play the piano and kiss you so's your hair'll uncurl and stick straight up in the air like a pickaninny." Well, boy, that girl laughed. Then she got shy. Started talkin' 'bout how Percy was too fast for her. She was talkin' alright, but Percy had pulled a string in her too. He left the troupe and stayed in Memphis. I didn't see Percy again, until '83 or '84, one. We teamed up and played the ends together. There was a lot of work for a colored man in minstrelsy in those days.

[**DOC:** It sure was. And '82 was the best, but those days are gone now.]

TAMBO: We was makin' 15, 20, 25, sometimes 35 dollars a week. A piece!

[**HENRY:** 35 dollars? Oh, sound like ya'll was in the big time.]

TAMBO: Seem like every penny Percy made, he either sent it to her or bought her somethin' with it. He was showin' this country girl a whole 'nother life she could only dream of. Only he didn't know he was primin' that well for somebody else to drink. We finished 6 weeks at Koster and Bial's. We had some time on our hands. Percy bought this solid gold wedding ring. Took me along for best man, and we started takin' trains to Memphis. That's when he started writing this song. On that train. All day and night on that clickety, clackity, rickety, rackity excuse for a train. With all the bumpin' and jerkin' he never took that paper out his lap or that pencil out his hand, 'til we got to Memphis. Boy, was he happy. He had done it. It was finished... She was waitin' for him at the station. Waitin' on him to lay it on him. There was another guy, she said. They was in love. They was already married. He was a school teacher. He was even there, standin' right down the other end of the platform

... Tall, skinny, yella nigga.

[**DOC:** A school teacher? Well, what happened then?]

TAMBO: Percy, a course, took it pretty bad. It was 'bout six months later, we walk into this theater in New Haven to see a minstrel show. There was this skit in the second part. The two white guys in the skit were blacked-up. One was dressed like a woman. Supposed to be a colored woman. The man was singin' the woman this song... It was Percy's song. It was bad enough that they was singin' the man's song, but the way they did it, was what made it so bad. A joke song, 'bout a couple a simple coons in love.

[**DOC:** How they get the song in the first place?]

TAMBO: I don't know, Doc. Seems like I got this picture in my mind a the last time I seen that song was crumpled up in Percy's fist. Or maybe it was blowin' away in the wind, skippin' down that platform and her chasin' after it. I guess she was kneeling down to pick it up, trying to straighten it out. I don't really remember.

45

MAN OF THE MOMENT
by Alan Ayckbourn

The pool area of a Mediterranean villa, the present
Vic Parks, a popular British talk show host, 40s
Vic here finds himself being interviewed for a competitor's
show, and offers the following dissertation on the fine art of
interviewing.

VIC: Well, he's really a stone mason. But he's had a spot of bother with the local law... No, the other thing you've got to remember about an interview is that, whoever's interviewing you will know less about what you're talking about than you do. Because nine times out of ten, he'll be talking to you about you – which makes you the resident expert, doesn't it? As far as you're concerned, it's a home game. He'll be nervous just coming down the tunnel, even before he's started. You see, there's an art to being interviewed. First, you've got to be able to use an interview to your own advantage. I mean, after all, what is an interview? This guy is more often than not trying to get you to say one thing – usually incriminating. And you, on the other hand, are wanting to say something of your own, entirely different to what he wants you to say. So it's a battle to the death, isn't it? If you're being interviewed, you have to turn it around, see? You say things like, "That's a very good question, John, and I'd like to answer it, if I may – with a question of my own." That always throws them, because they can't bear getting questions back at them. Because they're not usually geared for answers. Only for questions. Because they're interviewers, see, and not meant to have opinions. So they can't answer, anyway. But when they don't, that makes them look furtive. And when he does get a question in, if you don't like the one he's asked you, then give an answer to another one... And when he interrupts you – which he will do, once he realizes that you're giving him the wrong answer, you say to him, "I really must be allowed to answer this question in my own way, John, please." And look a bit hurt whilst you're saying it. 'Cause that'll make him look like a pushy bastard, too. And another tip, if you're giving an answer and you do happen to know the answer and don't mind giving it to him, talk as fast as you can while still making sense, but don't, whatever you do, leave pauses. Because they're looking for pauses, see, to edit you about and change your meaning. That's when they put in those nodding bits. You've seen them, when the bloke's nodding his head for dear life about bugger all and sitting in a different room. But if you don't pause, they can't get in to edit, can they? And if they can't edit you, they've either got to leave the interview out altogether, which means they haven't got a programme, which is generally disaster time, or they have to put in what you said in its entirety and not some version of what some monkey would have liked you to have said if he'd got the chance to edit you. And if you're in full flow and you do run out and you do have to stop, stop suddenly. Just like that. *(Quick pause.)* OK? Because that throws him as well. Because, nine out of ten, if it's a long answer you've been giving him, he won't be listening, anyway. He'll either be looking at his notes or at the floor manager, or wondering how long's this bleeder going in for? And if none of that works and you're really up against it, have a choking fit, throw yourself on the floor, knock the mike over and call for water. That usually does the trick.

MARINER
by Don Nigro

The flagship of Christopher Columbus, 1492
Ancient Mariner, an old salt, 50-80
As the men sailing on the first voyage of Columbus grumble
about not sighting land, the eldest of their number ruminates on their
special lot in life.

ANCIENT MARINER: *(Looking out.)* There are three types of people: the living, the dead and the sailors. The living are alive, the dead are dead, but the sailors are caught between, death all around, the deep ready to swallow them, one mis-step and they disappear forever beneath the cold water into fathomless darkness. And them that wait on shore can't know at any given time if the loved one's live or dead. They might be going about their daily tasks, imagining the beloved on his ship at sea, when all the while he's been rotting on the ocean floor, eyes picked out by crabs. Or they might have given him up for dead, then one day see him walking down the path to the house, shipwrecked young, returning old, with nothing in between but separation. A sailor's suspended like a dream between the light above and the dark below. He sails on unknown seas to an unknown destination, like everybody else, but for him the thing is simpler, is seen in its elemental elements. The way to get there is to set out and go, you'll eventually get someplace or other, probably not where you were aiming at, but there you are, the alternative is to go nowhere. I'm going to break wind like an old Scotch bagpipe.

MY SIDE OF THE STORY
by Bryan Goluboff

The bathroom of a luxury apartment in NYC, the present
Aaron, a young baron of Wall Street, 25
Aaron has just closed a $2 million deal for the family firm and
here brags to his father of his coup.

AARON: Are you ready for this? *(Aaron starts to unbutton his shirt.)* In your absence today, I made the company two million dollars. Curious? *(Gil doesn't say anything.)* I don't wanna tell you this through a door. *(Still no response; Aaron plunges on.)* Remember Michael Levine, my friend from Wharton? He's in M & A at Morgan Stanley now. This morning, he tipped me off that Stoneham Lumber was about to get an unfriendly bid from the Woodland Corporation. I went over to the Quotron and, sure enough, the stock was jumping like crazy. I was drooling like a fucking dog. So I went to Kilkenny and said, "Let's call and pitch the defense. This company's gonna get an offer." Well, Stoneham bit, they're sending their general counsel down from Virginia to meet with me tomorrow. You weren't there, man, I hadda pull the trigger. *(Still no response from Gil.)* Dad, can you hear me?

[**GIL:** Uh huh…]

AARON: I also called Henry Gottlieb, wet his beak a little. I know you owed him a favor for parking those stocks for you. I said, "Mr. Gottlieb, let's make some dough ray me!" He gobbled up 200,000 shares, bargain basement. We're gonna watch it soar all morning, then he's gonna take me to Harry's for steak and beer, 1 o'clock sharp. You're welcome to join us, if you'd like… *(Gil laughs sardonically to himself.)* I know it's dangerous, but we're not like those shmucks were at Drexel. Levine's slick as a pimp, he did everything in code, it's untraceable. Dad?

[**GIL:** I'm still here…]

AARON: You were looking for a sign from me. Well here it is. Like I said, maybe two million worth... *(Aaron takes off his shirt. He has a white t-shirt underneath. He looks like he spends many hours in the gym, lean and muscular.)* It's great to get in the ring for the first time and find out you can hit with both hands... *(Aaron sits down and takes off his shoes.)* I gotta get my shoes made custom, like yours. These are killing me... *(Aaron rubs his feet.)* Don't be pissed off, I took a car home from the gym and charged it to the company. I tried to take the subway, but the gate was down at the Wall Street station and all these extras from "Dawn of the Dead" were down there with their hands out. They're not so polite when it's dark. One guy was really pushing me. I said, "Get that styrofoam cup outta my face! I work hard for my money. You got two hands, get a job, push a broom." Well, I didn't say it, but I thought it... *(Pause.)* I can't believe you have nothing to say. I was all ready to do battle with you, Dad. I made a mockery of the rules. I played with real money...

MY SIDE OF THE STORY
by Bryan Goluboff

The bathroom of a luxury apartment in NYC, the present
Gil, a seasoned Wall Street player, 40-50
Gil has been drinking tequila in his bathroom all afternoon.
When he is discovered by his son, he explains that he fears that his wife is
having an affair.

GIL: Fuck man, I thought you'd help me...I really did... *(Gil takes a drink.)* I saw him touch her on the street, O.K.? I saw them together. He moved a lock of her hair out of her face in such a way that... Oh, Aaron...I felt... Can I talk to you...? Shit... *(Gil tries to find the right words.)* I started to picture it, I didn't want to, but it just came up – her unwrapped on the bed like a birthday gift, him on top of her, his scrawny fucking ass, doing things, he's got some kind of magic... Then it's black, you know, like murder. The end. They call me "The Killer" downtown, you know that? 'Cause when I snap, things change...

[**AARON:** Tell me what happened...]

GIL: I found myself outside this restaurant. They're sitting in the window. She's smiling like high school... I'm sweating behind this bush, hiding... Finally, I went inside... *(Gil takes a deep breath.)* I went up to the table. They were shocked to see me. They sounded like the record was on the wrong speed – excuses, excuses. I didn't hear a word. They shut up. I didn't know if I was gonna smash his face or scratch her skin off her... I reached over onto his plate and picked up this huge piece of steak and I – *(He shows Aaron how he tore the steak to pieces right in front of their faces. It is a strangely violent and vicious act, especially with the vigor that Gil pantomimes it.)* Ripped it apart. Blood splattered everywhere, on my shirt, in your mother's face... It was weird, I don't know why I did that... The restaurant was silent. I mean, nothing... And I came to. Just snapped out of it. Regained control. Your mother was crying, wiping that blood off her face. And I ran out of the restaurant, I ran for blocks… Thinking, "Sucker, sucker, sucker, you shoulda known…

[**AARON:** Jesus Christ, that's crazy. That's a crazy thing to do. But you didn't really hurt anybody, right?]

GIL: I'm so stupid –

ONE THING IS NOT ANOTHER
(A VAUDEVILLE)
by Kenneth Bernard

Here and now
Old Man, an old man in a wheelchair, 60+
Here, an old man shares a sad memory about a family pet.

OLD MAN: He was as nice a dog as a boy could have. Smelled, of course, and not handsome or anything. But sweet as could be, and took abuse kindly, too. He was really my best friend then, and slept with me in every season, snoring to beat the band and twitching like mad. Oh, I loved Rex, let me tell you. And vomited right off when I saw him that morning, his head beaten in, whimpering. He snapped at first, not being able to see. But when he heard my voice and felt my hand he calmed down. I cradled his head in my lap and cried while Dad went for help. But it wasn't any good. Rex couldn't make it. He died there, me holding him. We found the bloody rock out by the road, and we knew who had wielded it, no stranger, and I wanted to kill him with the same rock. But Dad said no, it was for other people to take care of. I was angry with him, thought him a coward. I still don't really know. I guess he was right. But nothing ever happened. We lived just down the road from Rex's killer for fourteen more years, and I hated him every one of them. Sometimes I thought he smiled at me. A few times I cried, waking up at night. And I still think of bashing his head in with a rock, wherever he is.

PILL HILL
by Samuel L. Kelley

A basement apartment in a tenement on Chicago's
South side, 1973
Al, a real estate salesman, African-American, 23-33
Following a domestic squabble, Al shares his angst with his buddies.

AL: Yeah – had a knock-down-drag-out fight with my old lady. She tells me she's got to have a four-bedroom house and a brand new Firebird. "Four bedrooms, baby! We got me and you and two kids. What we need with four bedrooms?" "We got to have an extra bedroom for the visiting kinfolk."

[**CHARLIE:** Time for somebody to start moonlighting?]

AL: I told her if she wants all that I got to be more than a two-bit inspector at the mill and she's gonna be doing something else beside standing behind a cosmetic counter in a downtown department store pushing perfume bottles under people's noses and smearing war paint on their faces.

[**JOE:** It's makeup, Al.]

AL: It's horse manure and I'm tired of rubbing my nose in it! *(Reaches in his coat pocket and pulls out a handful of cut-up credit cards.)* Look at this! *(And flings them around room.)* Goddamn *credit* cards! "I know your black ass lying now!" "Yes I am. The hell if you charging my ass into the grave!" "Nigger, get you black hands out of my purse before I break um off!" *(To others.)* I'm not owing my soul to these department stores any longer. Takes damn near a whole year to pay off the Christmas bills. "We got big families to buy presents for Christmas." "Let them eat turkey and sweet potato pie." *(Pulling more cards from his pocket.)* I ask her, "Where the hell did you think we were going when we got married, woman?" "We got married because I was five months pregnant and we were trying to make it to the altar before my daddy lynched your ass." "Okay, okay," I told her, " but it's gonna be a cold day in hell when number three get here." *(Shaking head in astonishment.)* Whew! Then she scared the shit out of my ass. "It might be on the way now for all you know." "YOU BETTER STOP IT IF HE IS!" We are both bright and intelligent people. Four, maybe five years from now, we could be through college. I told her that. She looks at me. "You might find yourself marching down that aisle *solo!*" *(With measured, provocative tone.)* I told her: "That ain't no big deal, baby, 'cause I'm MARCHING DOWN THAT AISLE BY MYSELF, OR WITH SOMEBODY ELSE IF I HAVE TO."

[**JOE:** That's when the pots and pans starting coming after your ass.]

AL: *(Amused relief.)* She went for the frying pans; I left for the party!

PILL HILL
by Samuel L. Kelley

A basement apartment in a tenement on Chicago's
South side, 1973
Charlie, a steel mill worker for 20 years, African-American, 42-52
At the prodding of his friends, Charlie here tells a horrific tale
of racism and violence which occurred when he and his wife and children
drove from Chicago to Mississippi for a family visit.

CHARLIE: *(Uneasy laughter.)* Figured all I had to do was put on my Stepin Fetchit mask when I got to Cairo, Illinois and I'd be home free. *(Others are amused.)* See, I didn't worry about the people sitting in, marching through water hoses, police dogs, getting shot, murdered while they sat in church shouting and praising the Lord. I had my Cadillac – hell, I had Cadillac immunity! Pulled up in front of my kinfolks' house – whole lot of um scrambling to "RIDE IN COUSIN CHARLIE'S CADILLAC!" They wanted to come back to Chicago. Bet you I cruised to the grocery store a dozen times before noonday – showing off my Cadillac. I got my wife and two boys and headed over to Smithville so Mama and Daddy could show the neighbors how fine their boy from up North was doing – 'twas near 'bout sundown. The MAN pulled up beside me – lights flashing! "Pull off the highway behind me at this here next road, boy." Wasn't speeding. Hell, I's cruising! Pulled off behind them. Flashed my gold teeth. Far as I's concerned I had Cadillac immunity. *(Spurt of painful and bitter laughter. Proceeding with painful difficulty.)* They got out – walked back to my car. "Boy, where you get this here car?" "Bought it." "Whatcha buy it wid?" "My money." "Got us a smart nigger from up North on our hands. Been running all over town in this here car, boy." "Beg your pardon?" "Nigger, my partner said ya been running your black ass all over town in this here goddamn car!" "Down here to stir up trouble?" "Nope, won't be no trouble from me if…" "Boy, did I hear you say, 'No, sir?'" "I don't remember." "Get your ass out the car, nigger!" "Gonna refresh your MEMORY." "Get your ass out the car, nigger!" "Over in front of this police car." "On your knees, boy!" *(Struggling, painfully.)* Got down on my... They stepped up – one on each side – stuck both pistols behind my ears. Cocked the pistols! "Clean off them headlights." "Touch um wid ya hands and I'll splatter ya colored brains from here to Chicago." I started licking – grime, grit, bugs. Licked um clean. "You forgot the other side, BOY!" "Start licking, nigger!" I licked them – clean. *(With unbearable difficulty.)* Bertha hid my sons' faces in her bosom. "Stand your black ass up." "Drop your pants." I hedged. One of um's foot knocked my ass out of kilter. Dropped my pants. Tall lanky one pulled out a hunting knife. "Drop your goddamn drawers." "HUH?" "Your drawers, NIGGER! YOUR GODDAMN DRAWERS!" Dropped my underwear. He stepped up behind me. "Grab your toes." "Your toes, NIGGER!" I... I... gra...grabbed my toes... fe...felt his knife against my balls. "Cough, nigger!" *(Coughs delicately, as though knife is against his balls.)* "Louder!" *(Louder, but delicately.)* "Louder, nigger!" *(Again, delicately.)* "This ain't gonna do." "Make the nigger sneeze." "Take a deep breath, boy!" "GUT-BUSTING SNEEZE, NIGGER!" *(At the point of sneezing, Charlie gives a loud spurt of angry, bitter laughter.)* Broke down crying. Bastards had me where they wanted me. Took my money, threw my wallet at me. "Boy, don't let sunup catch your black ass in this town." "Hear what the man said, NIGGER!" "YESSIR!" *(With much relief.)* Next morning – saw that Chicago skyline rising to meet me. Parked that Cadillac. Washed it. Waxed it. Pulled it up in the garage. Jacked it up on four blocks. To hell with that Cadillac! Looking out for my family and getting them a home and making sure my boys would never see me on my knees licking the MAN's headlights was the most important thing in my life! I got me a second job – moonlighting janitor – fifteen years I did. *(With affection.)* Bertha, she went to work... we cooked that old Irish potato more ways than the good Lord counted days in the month. "What's for dinner, honey?" "Chicken pot pie, baby!" "I'm into my second helping – ain't found a piece of chicken, sweetheart..." *(To others, with amusement.)* Helluva lot of ways to cook beans and corn bread...

IT'S RALPH
by Hugh Whitemore

A country cottage, England, the present
Andrew, a television personality, 50
In the middle of a philosophical discussion of the nature of truth,   down-
to-earth Andrew reveals a near-sordid event from his childhood.

ANDREW: Father Prideaux was the local priest, we were living in
Bristol at the time; Prideaux, E-A-U-X, youngish, rather jolly. I was
about fourteen. Earnest and spotty. Mad about culture. A real
herbert. Father Prideaux offered to take me to London to see an
exhibition – Henry Moore at the Tate. My old Mum was thrilled to
bits; Father Prideaux could do no wrong in her eyes, she thought
he came from a good family; she was frightfully keen on good
families, coming from a lousy one herself. So off we went, Father
Prideaux and I, off to the Tate Gallery. On the way home, he put
his hand on my flies – buttons in those days, don't forget. We
were sitting side-by-side in the empty carriage, rattling through
Chippenham. Well I was tremendously shocked; not so much by
the attempted seduction, which was tentative and half-hearted in
the extreme, but because I thought his mind should've been on
higher things. And he was risking so much, after all: disgrace, de-
frocking (whatever they call it), hell-fire and eternal damnation, to
name but a few. Was my pubescent cock worth more to Father
Prideaux than his relationship with Almighty God? Obviously yes.
Well that made God look pretty silly, it also got me thinking – fatal
– and the more I thought the less I believed. Eventually, of course,
I stopped going to church. Mum was dreadfully upset. Auntie Peg
wrote to me from her shrine in Peckham. "Your mother's heart is
broken," she said. "I shall pray that your faith shall be restored to
you." Her prayers went unanswered. God turned a deaf ear – if
God has ears. I wonder if he has, do you think? I wonder if there's
a theological preposition about that, do you suppose? (Glancing at
Clare.) What's the matter? Why are you looking at me like that?

[**CLARE:** You evade everything. Everything has to be a joke.]

ANDREW: Nothing wrong with jokes. A good joke is truth without pain. "Why is a blow-job like lobster thermidor?" "You don't get either at home." The sexual impoverishment of ten million marriages is contained within that joke. Far more penetrating than any sociological survey, and certainly more succinct.

IT'S RALPH
by Hugh Whitemore

A country cottage, England, the present
Dave, a carpenter, 20 When a tragic accident claims the life of Andrew's
old friend, he calls his wife, only to discover that she is in bed with
another man. He turns to Dave for sympathy, and instead is treated to the
following story from Dave's childhood.

DAVE: Poor old Ralph. I'd never seen anyone dead before. *(Pause.)* Actually that's not true. There was someone. When I was a kid. My Dad's auntie. She was funny in the head. She thought she could flap her arms up and down and fly like a bird. They had her put away. But then, when she got older, Dad thought she should come and live with us. We had a house out in the country, in Essex. Dad thought she should end her days with the family and not in a loony bin. The house was very unusual. Tall and thin. And there was trees all 'round it. There was a gap in the trees, and through that gap you could see the Colchester to London railway line. My old aunt loved to watch the trains go by. They gave her a room on the top floor so she could see the trains clearly. They kept the window locked, just in case. One day she managed to prise the window open. She crawled onto the window sill, flapped her arms up and down, and jumped. Poor old darling. Mum rushed out and found her. "Don't look," she said, but of course I did. Wasn't nasty or frightening. Just a funny bundle of clothes with legs and arms sticking out of it. Mum said it was a blessed release. She often said that about people dying. *(Pause.)* I suppose some people thought she killed herself because we kept her locked up and were cruel to her. Perhaps some people thought she was trying to escape and killed herself accidentally. Some people knew the truth, of course. And perhaps there was someone in a train going from Colchester to London. And perhaps he looked out of the window, and perhaps, through that gap in the trees, he saw an old lady in mid-air, flapping her arms up and down. Just for a split-second, as the train rushed on, past our house. And he'd look through the window, that man, and he'd be amazed. He'd tell his friends, "I saw an old lady flying," he'd say. So, in a way, it actually happened. What she wanted. Perhaps she died happy. What do you think?

THE RESURRECTION OF DARK SOLDIERS
by William Electric Black

An apartment in NYC, the present
Ujamma, a homeless Vietnam vet, African-American, 40s
This wandering vet is a desolate voice in the wilderness
expressing years of frustration and dispair.

UJAMMA: *(Distantly.)* Homeless Black folk gather. We sleep in subway cars, on beaches, in the gutters, in boxes over hot air vents… any hooch we can find.

We smell of urine, wine, vomit. The old Black men … the young ones. The women, most of them raped, stand not far away. *(Pause.)*

We all gather around a crackling fire during a cold night. The flames remind me of exploding satchel charges from some stinking sapper who had got into our base. *(To George X.)*

We can make no demands… we who have no home, no family, no job. We who live from dime to dime, surviving the best we can. Hoping to beat the weather that might freeze us…or a can of lighter fluid that might set us ablaze. *(He begins to move about.)*

GOD… I'M ON FIRE! GOD…HELP ME! The sound of an AK-47 rock 'n rolling makes me dance a thousand times better than James Brown. GOD…I'M SWEATING! Like I would at a Saturday afternoon barbecue. *(Pause.)*

Over at the card table some gin drinking brothers argue about a card game. Johnny Mack tells Otis he's cheating. Nigger say, "YOU LYING…YOU LYING BASTARD!" Johnny Mack pulls out his piece but Otis shoots him first. JOHNNY MACK IS DEAD! HE'S DEAD! A pool of blood becomes the only pool Johnny Mack would swim in that day. *(Pause.)*

The crackling fire begins to die. The firefight is over. We without shelter begin to fade. Ashes to ashes. Dust to dust. Who *cares* about our demands?

THE REVENGER'S COMEDIES
by Alan Aykbourn

A gymkhana, the present
Anthony Staxton-Brilling, a superficial boor, 38
When confronted with his infidelity while watching a gymkhana,
Anthony reveals his callous nature.

ANTHONY: Karen Knightly and I had – well, you could hardly term it an affair – had a bit of sex together, let's say – for all of a month. Well, quite a lot of sex, really. We tried out all twenty-five of the bedrooms in that house of hers over the course of about a fortnight, starting in the attic and finishing up in the master suite. She insisted we dressed in suitable clothes to suit different locations. I remember our night in the nursery as particularly bizarre. When we'd completed the course, she declared that according to ancient law we were now legally engaged. And that at the next full moon I had to sacrifice my existing wife Imogen and change my name to Alric the Awesome. At which point, I realized I was stark staring mad and I broke off the relationship. She then plagued us both for months. Writing anonymous letters, drawing strange runes on our front door, phoning up claiming to be a midwife delivering my illegitimate child. You name it, she did it. Culminating, finally, in a phone call demanding that I be on Chelsea Bridge at eight thirty sharp or she would throw herself in the Thames.

[**HENRY:** *(Suspecting a ring of truth in all this.)* My God. And did you go?]

ANTHONY: Yes, I did. I stood on that bloody bridge for an hour and half hoping to see her jump. No such luck. Not so much as a ripple. So I went home again.

SIGHT UNSEEN
by Donald Margulies

An art gallery in London, the present
When Jonathan, a highly regarded artist, visits London, he is
interviewed by a German reporter for an art magazine. During
their conversation, he offers the following dissertation on the
state of art and the media.

JONATHAN: Okay, let me ask you something: When *we* talk about good art, what are we talking about? Stuff we like? Stuff our friends make? We're talking about value judgments. Most people, do you think most people, most Americans – my *father* – do you think most people have any idea what makes good art?

[**GRETE:** Hm.]

JONATHAN: The little old lady who paints flowers and pussycats at the YMCA – and *dazzles* her friends, I'm sure – I mean, does that little old lady make good art? I mean, why not? Her cat looks just *like* that. I'm not putting her down; I think it's great she's got a hobby. But is what she does good art? See, most people...

I remember, years ago, the big van Gogh show at the Met?, in New York? The place was packed. Like Yankee Stadium. Buses emptied out from all over: Jersey, Westchester. All kinds of people. The masses. Average middle-class people. Like they were coming into the city for a matinee and lunch at Mamma Leone's. Only this was Art. Art with a capital A had come to the shopping mall generation and Vincent was the chosen icon. Now, I have nothing against van Gogh. Better him than people lining up to see the kids with the big eyes. But as I braved that exhibit – and it was rough going, believe me – I couldn't help but think of Kirk Douglas. Kirk Douglas should've gotten a cut of the house.

See, there's this Hollywood packaging of the artist that gets me.

The packaging of the mystique. Poor, tragic Vincent: he cut off his ear 'cause he was so misunderstood but still he painted all these pretty pictures. So ten bodies deep they lined up in front of the paintings. More out of solidarity for Vincent (or Kirk) than out of any kind of love or passion for "good art." Hell, some art lovers were in such a hurry to get to the postcards and prints and souvenir placemats, they strode past the paintings and skipped the show entirely! Who can blame them? You couldn't *experience* the paintings anyway, not like that. You couldn't *see* anything. The art was just a backdrop for the *real* show that was happening. In the gift shop!

[**GRETE:** Hm.]

JONATHAN: Now, you got to admit there's something really strange about all this, this kind of *frenzy* for art. I mean, what *is* this thing called art? What's it for? Why have people historically drunk themselves to death over the creation of it, or been thrown in jail, or whatever? I mean, how does it serve the masses? *Can* it serve the – I ask myself these questions all the time. Every painting I do is another attempt to come up with some answers. The people who crowded the Met to look at sunflowers, I mean, why *did* they? 'Cause they *thought* they should. 'Cause they thought they were somehow enriching their lives. Why? *'Cause the media told them so!*

A SLIP OF THE TONGUE
by Dusty Hughes

A meeting of the Writer's Union, the Soviet Union, 1969
Tantra, a dissident writer, 20s
Here, young Tantra addresses the Writer's Union one last time
before his censure.

TANTRA: Thank you for giving me this opportunity of addressing you for the last time, colleagues of The Writer's Union. *(Pause.)* In one of the least amusing books ever written by a psychoanalyst, Freud analyses the technique of the Joke. When I thought about this book, I began to think about you, my soon to be ex-colleagues. I think it's a book you can profitably study. *(He solemnly puts on a clown's red nose.)* Freud begins by offering us the dictum: "Freedom produces Jokes, and Jokes produce Freedom." In my opinion this is half true and half a lie. Which half is true and which a lie, I will leave you to argue about. Of course, dear friends, jokes are entirely subjective. They may also lose a great deal in translation. The cry *"Tradutore – traditore!"* is an Italian example of one of the simplest of all jokes which rely on the modification of words. "Translator – traitor!" More challenging is an example of what Freud calls the "Condensation with Modification" joke. The very title makes the blood freeze... for example, Mr. X was made Minister of Agriculture. His only qualification being that he himself lives on a farm. When his colleagues in the government were at last forced to admit that X was a very bad choice, he resigned and returned to his estate. It was said, in jest, that Mr. X had, like the Roman Cinciratus, "gone back to his place *behind* the plough" and that what went before the plough in Roman times, as in Freud's own, was an ox. *(Pause.)* But enough of the Condensation with Modification joke. *(Pause.)* Here's another good one. A young man was introduced into a Paris salon. He was a relative of the great philosopher Jean Jacques Rousseau. He was red haired and very nervous. In fact he behaved so stupidly that the hostess remarked to the man who had introduced him, "You have brought me a man who is *roux* (red)

65

and *sot* (stupid) but not a Rousseau." This is an example of *Klangwitz*. That is the joke that relies for it's brilliance on the *sound* of the words. It would not take much imagination, Mr. Chairman, to see that if I substituted your own name, Wallenstein, into the joke, things would be very different. "You have brought me a man who is *roux* and *sot* ... but not a Wallenstein." Not much of a joke. Which is why I suppose none of you are laughing. Friends, please do feel free not to laugh. This is a serious investigation into the Technique of the Joke and no one should feel obliged to merely fall about. We'll deal with irony some other time. *(Pause.)* The jokes we have discussed so far have been what one might call the Innocent or Pure Joke. The Joke, as it were, for Joke's sake. But what about the joke of substance, the joke of deeper meaning. But, oh... *"Tradutore – traditore!,"* while the joke asserts something of great value it may not actually be funny. Take the statement that not everyone who makes fun of his chains is actually free. Pungent. But do we actually laugh? If I referred to the recent job I had in the lavatories of the Central Station by saying "experience is all about experiencing what one does not wish to experience"... *(Pause.)* you may find it very funny. You do find it very funny. Though in fact the statement is really rather trite. Experience is all about experiencing what one does not wish to experience. *(Pulls a face.)* Poetry can transform triteness of course. "Sweet are the uses of adversity!" How noble. But how often a downright lie. Adversity is seldom if ever sweet. I knew a family here in our lovely old city and they themselves were fond of telling jokes. Whenever you called on them they were always at it. Jokes, jokes, jokes ... And they owned an Amazonian parrot. One day the parrot got out of it's cage and pissed off out of the window to freedom. The family didn't bother to look for it, instead they went straight off to the secret police. "Why come to us?" the officer said. "Nobody's handed in a parrot here." "Well," said my friends, "it's bound to end up here sooner or later and we want you to know that we don't agree with a word it says." Thank you!

THOU SHALT WISE UP
by Kelly Masterson

God's waiting room, Heaven, the present
Joe Humboldt, a simple man with faith in God, 30-50
When Humboldt finds himself in God's waiting room, he makes
the following introduction in which he reveals his rather
Job-like tendencies.

HUMBOLDT: Is anyone here? My name is Joe Humboldt. Am I in heaven? I am prepared to make my final accounting. Is anyone listening? Of course you're listening, aren't you, God? If I had to choose one word to describe my life, it would be faith. I lived a life of faith. My parents died in an automobile crash on the way to the hospital to have me. I was raised in an orphanage with mean Catholic nuns. I ate gruel and wore rags but the sisters instilled in me a faith so strong, it would not bend. At fourteen, I ran away from the orphanage and worked on the docks in Boston. I worked 12 hours a day and earned just enough to feed myself. At night I'd wander South Boston where I was mugged and beaten and raped with regularity. I slept in a large steel drum under a bridge for three years. I remember feeling that the drum was like my faith – a strong, outer shell that would protect me. At 17, I joined the army and served four years in Nam. I saw good men die; I saw horror; I saw the face of hell. My life was spared and I came to believe that God was protecting me, saving me for something important. I lost a leg in a mine explosion – this one, no … Yeah, this one, though now it feels like flesh and blood again. It took a fake leg and a year of physical therapy but I walked out of that hospital with God on my shoulder and a song of praise in my heart. I found a job driving a school bus for handicapped children in Syracuse. I was falsely accused of child molestation and sentenced to twenty years in Sing Sing. In Sing Sing I was continually mugged and beaten and raped. I lost my other leg – this one – or, what does it matter? On the day I was to be paroled, I was informed that the prison computer had eaten my records and was forced to begin my twenty years again. I managed a daring escape, threatening to hit a guard with one of my fake legs. I wouldn't really have used my leg in an act of violence – I have never raised a leg against any man. I was struck by lightning and lost an eye. I contracted polio and lost the use of both arms. I lived in a cardboard box in Bakersfield. I got scarlet fever and lost my hearing. I ate worms and insects and lived in a cattle car on the Atchison, Topeka and the Santa Fe where I was beaten and mugged and raped repeatedly. I was in a terrifying train wreck and lost a lung and my sense of smell. While in the hospital, I was accidentally given chemotherapy. I lost my hair and contracted leukemia. I lost my appetite. I lost weight. I lost the lottery. But through it all, I never lost my faith. The doctor who diagnosed my multiple sclerosis said I was a modern Job. Or maybe he said, "a modern joke." – I never really got the hang of lip reading. I don't know if I was Job or not, but I do know that nothing shook my faith. Every test, every tribulation, every lost limb only served to strengthen my belief in a loving God who would welcome me gladly into his kingdom. *(The television set comes on.)*

And so I enter his glory and claim my just reward.

THREE BIRDS ALIGHTING ON A FIELD
by Timberlake Wertenbaker

An artist's studio, the present
Constantin, a Romanian visiting London, 30-50
This enigmatic Romanian has been circulating to London's art circles for
several weeks attempting to persuade artists to donate their work to his
country. When his motives are finally questioned, he lashes out fiercely
against the world that deserted his country in its darkest hour.

CONSTANTIN: Yes, I understand. I – we disappoint you. We are
not doing things right, we are not pure. The trouble for us is we
have to carry your dreams, your ideals, always. You were on the
left in your country, no? That's what I thought. You are the worst.
I don't mind the silly society ladies – I never really expected to get
help from them because we Romanians are not chic, I know that.
But you – you never came to Romania when we were communist.
You preach communism in your country, but you let us make the
experiment for you. So we have the destroyed land in co-
operatives, the bread tails, but it doesn't matter, because we are
your ideal. And when it has completely failed, and we have a
revolution, you love us because we are having a revolution and
that is exciting to you, even if it is a revolution against what you
are preaching for in your country. And again we carry your soul for
you. And now you're unhappy because we are not perfect
revolutionaries, because we have not wiped out all the Securitate
people, which is most of Romanians, because we are not
completely good. You forgive your own evil because you say it's
built into capitalism, but we are not allowed. We have to be
moral, perfect martyrs.

     You come and watch us, you say we are not good to our
babies. You want us to have habits like people who have been
well fed, with love, with toys, things we never know about and we
are just so happy we are not under Ceausescu, that is enough for
us, that we are less frightened. Now you don't want me to have
your paintings because I am not great dissident hero. Where were
you when they were beating and killing us? You despise me
because I want to live. You, socialist? I go walk in the garden now.

TWO SHAKESPEAREAN ACTORS
by Richard Nelson

Various locations in New York City, May, 1849
William Charles Macready, an English actor performing
in New York, 40-50 When Macready meets his American counterpart,
Edwin Forrest, the dinner conversation gets interesting. When Forrest asks
Macready why he acts, the veteran performer offers the following
explanation.

MACREADY: It's hard to explain really. Where shall I begin? *(Beat.)* You see – as Descartes has said – inside us all are these – He called them animal spirits. *(Beat.)* Which are really, what other people call – passions. *(Short pause. Forrest nods.)* And they're all – these spirits – they're bordered, they're all sort of fenced in. *(Suddenly remembering.)* You could also call them *emotions*. *(Beat.)* Anyway, they're fenced in. But when one of them escapes from the others – and is not quickly caught by – I don't know, spirits who do the catching, like sheep dogs catch – *(Beat.)*

[**FORREST:** Sheep.]

MACREADY: That's right. Like sheep dogs catch sheep. Anyway, when one escapes and is not caught, then it becomes a very deep, a very – a very passionate – *(Beat.)* What?! *(Beat. Remembers.)* Feeling! Feeling. *(Short pause.)* So what an actor does – I believe – is this: philosophically speaking – . I haven't studied enough philosophy–. I'd like to study much more, but–. Well –. People like us who are busy *doing* –! But, as I was saying, the art of the actor –. *(Beat.)* What was I going to say? I was about to say something that was very clear. I remember. The art of the actor is like ripping down fences. *(Beat.)* And tying up the sheep dogs. *(Beat.)* And letting the spirits loose. A few at a time. Or more! Depending on the part. Letting them roam for a while. *(Short pause.)* So, that's what I love about acting. *(Pause.)* I don't know how clear I've been.

TWO SHAKESPEAREAN ACTORS
by Richard Nelson

Various locations in New York City, May, 1849
William Charles Macready, an English actor performing
in New York, 40-50
When Macready's New York performance of *Macbeth* causes a riot, he
suffers from nightmares which he here shares with his assistant.

MACREADY: I'm going to smell for days. *(Smiles.)* My spit will intoxicate at least the first three rows. *(Wider smile. Ryder brings him a drink. He sips.)* It was an actor's dream. John.
[**RYDER:** Not surprising.]
MACREADY: The actor's dream. *(Beat.)* Do cobblers and coat-makers have their dreams? One wonders. Though mine was an interesting variation. It wasn't that I could not remember my lines or what part I was playing or which play I was in. Rather – it was the reverse. *(Beat.)* In my dream, I was speaking all the parts. One second I was – whatever. I can't remember. Then the next, I was speaking back to me. Then entering to tell me something. Then telling me to leave so I could be alone and have my soliloquy. *(Beat.)* Rather exhausting this was. And rather unnerving to the other actors whose parts I was obviously usurping. Thus one by one they – my fellow actors – retreated from the stage and allowed me to be alone with various other mes. *(Beat.)* One or two left quite angrily too. This I could not understand. After all, I was much better than they could ever hope to be. They should have appreciated this. *(Short pause.)* When it came for Macduff to kill Macbeth – so obviously this was *Macbeth* – I found myself in a quandary, of course. *(Laughs to himself.)* The audience was cheering. They screamed. Were they praising my performance? Were they after my death? I did not understand the effect I was having. *(Beat.)* And then – as the script calls for it – I killed myself, or rather my Macduff killed my Macbeth. And the pain, it was horrific. *(Short pause. Looks at Ryder.)* I knew every part and was good. *(Laughs. Beat.)* I shall be afraid to sleep again The sun should be up when? *(Ryder shrugs.)*

UNFINISHED STORIES
by Sybille Pearson

New York City, present
Walter, 80
Walter is discussing his grandson Daniel's future with him.
Daniel drives a cab but fantasizes a life in the country raising
Christmas trees. He disavows religion when Walter is surprised
at the choice of Christmas trees. Walter lectures Daniel.

WALTER: My boy. *(He gestures Daniel closer to him.)* My father would say, if a policeman asks your religion, you say Jew. This was before Hitler. Do not say to the policeman we are agnostics. He will spit and say, "you dirty Jew, you try to ingratiate yourself with us." We do not give him that satisfaction. But to a Jew also say Jew. If you say we are agnostics, he will spit and say, "you Jew hater. Selbtshasser." No matter there hadn't been a God in the house for four generations. I thought my father a coward. I said to all what I was. Agnostic. My father stayed in Berlin. He was murdered as a Jew. So I say I am a Jew. Without a God and now with a Christmas tree. And I like it. I like to think of you in the country. Yes.

UNFINISHED STORIES
by Sybille Pearson

New York City, present
Yves, 45-50
Walter, Daniel's grandfather, has just died. Daniel tells his father,
Yves, after the funeral that he fears he let the old man down at
the end. Yves, whose relationship with Walter was never
resolved, speaks to Daniel.

YVES: *(Grabs Daniel.)* Let him into your heart. Never into your head.

[**DANIEL:** I loved him.]

YVES: And you showed it and that's no failure. And stood up for him. That's no failure.

[**DANIEL:** But you don't know…]

YVES: I know this! It's our story. His, yours, mine! I know the day you learned it. When you were this big. In here. In this room. Passed from hand to hand. Your crib was there. This was yours before he moved in. Before my mother died. And she was here. Everyone was. Everyone held you, looked at you and then said something about you, and passed you on to the next person. It seemed like the school game where one starts a story and the next adds to it and the next till it gets an ending. When Walter held you out to me… O nouveau-ne, this amazing new life… Gaby thought it was that I was afraid I'd drop you. No. My hands shook because it was as though he was handing me a story, the story he and I hadn't finished, which he hadn't   finished with his father, that I swore would have an ending before I ever ever had a child. You understand. The failure is ours. The apology is ours. Is mine.

WHAT IS THIS EVERYTHING?
by Patricia Scanlon

A coffee shop, late at night, present
The Waiter, a pragmatic guy, 50-60
Waiter gets fed up with young man and woman who have been
at his counter, drinking coffee and philosophizing, all day. He
drives them out, explodes and then does some philosophizing
of his own.

WAITER: Let me tell you something. I got two. That's right, two jobs. One in the morning. One at night. And I never missed a day a work in my life. Sometimes I'm pushin' say sixty, seventy hours a week. Someone offers me overtime, I take it. And you, look at you. You're sitting around scratchin' your fat "arse," looking for the "meaning of life." You get up, you do what you gotta do, then you go to bed knowing you done it. That's it. And every once in a while you buy yourself a nice meal. A steak. Lobster. Something nice. And a bottle-a-beer for two. That's it, that's life. Burns me up. Burns my arse see a young man like you sittin' around wasting his life. Sitting around with a big fat hair across his arse "thinki-i-in" about "things." Just looking for something not to agree with. While I'm out busting my arse and then paying taxes up the wazoo taboot to support people like you. *(Including Trash in this now.)* Freeloaders who refuse to live in the real world like the rest of us. Well, I got news for you, your ka-ka stinks like everyone else's, *(To Trash.)* no offense. And I got even bigger news for the both of you – it takes real money to live in either world. World full of people like you, the world would go to hell in a hand-barrel before you could blink an eye. A world full of "THINK-A-A-AS." A world full of "poets." Now that's something to think about.